NOTHING
EXCEPT OURSELVES

NOTHING
EXCEPT OURSELVES

VIKING

The Harsh Times
and Bold Theater of
South Africa's
MBONGENI NGEMA

Laura Jones

VIKING
Published by the Penguin Group
Penguin Books USA Inc., 375 Hudson Street,
New York, New York 10014, U.S.A.
Penguin Books Ltd, 27 Wrights Lane,
London W8 5TZ, England
Penguin Books Australia Ltd, Ringwood,
Victoria, Australia
Penguin Books Canada Ltd, 10 Alcorn Avenue,
Toronto, Ontario, Canada M4V 3B2
Penguin Books (N.Z.) Ltd, 182–190 Wairau Road,
Auckland 10, New Zealand

Penguin Books Ltd, Registered Offices:
Harmondsworth, Middlesex, England

First published in 1994 by Viking Penguin,
a division of Penguin Books USA Inc.

1 3 5 7 9 10 8 6 4 2

Grateful acknowledgment is made for permission to reprint excerpts from the following copy-righted works:

"The Portuguese Sea" from *Fernando Pessoa: Sixty Portuguese Poems* translated by F. E. G. Quintanilha, University of Wales Press, 1973. By permission of the publisher.

Woza Albert! by Percy Mtwa, Mbongeni Ngema, and Barney Simon. Copyright © 1982 by Percy Mtwa, Mbongeni Ngema, and Barney Simon. Published in Great Britain by Methuen London Ltd. Reprinted by permission of George Braziller, Inc.

Laura Jones's interview with Peter Brook in *The New Theater Review.* © 1988 The New Theater Review, a Lincoln Center Theater publication.

Asinamali! by Mbongeni Ngema. Copyright © 1986 by Mbongeni Ngema. Reprinted by permission of George Braziller, Inc.

"After the Death of Mdabuli" by Mazisi Kunene. By permission of Mazisi Kunene.

LIBRARY OF CONGRESS CATALOGING IN PUBLICATION DATA
Jones, Laura.
Nothing except ourselves: the harsh times and bold theater
of South Africa's Mbongeni Ngema/by Laura Jones.
p.   cm.
Includes index.
ISBN 0–670–83619–2
1. Ngema, Mbongeni. 2. Dramatists, South African—20th century—Biography.
3. Theater—South Africa—History—20th century. 4. Blacks—South Africa—Intellectual
life. 5. South Africa—In literature. 6. Blacks in literature.   I. Title.
PR9369.N44Z73   1994
822—dc20   94-33333

This book is printed on acid-free paper.

Printed in the United States of America
Set in Simoncini Garamond
Designed by Kathryn Parise

To my grandmother,
Florence Price
▼

PREFACE

▼

Mbongeni Ngema first came to America in 1982, with *Woza Albert!,* a play that he and Percy Mtwa acted in and co-wrote with fellow South African Barney Simon. Ngema toured with that production throughout America and internationally for some five years. I didn't meet him until 1986, when his next piece of work, *Asinamali!*—which he himself wrote and directed but did not act in—came to New York at the start of another prolonged international tour, culminating on Broadway. The performance I saw of *Asinamali!,* its first in America, at the Roger Furman Theatre in Harlem, lasts in my mind as one of the most electrifying experiences I've had in the theater. I had never seen a play that could be, in the exact same moment, so wrenchingly painful and so fiercely joyous.

At the time, I was working at Lincoln Center Theater, where we were preparing to produce a festival of South African plays slated to open, a few months later, with *Asinamali!* My bosses, Gregory Mosher and Bernard Gersten, so admired *Asinamali!* and so strongly believed in Ngema that they offered to produce his next play, *Sarafina!,* before they'd seen it—before, indeed, Ngema had even begun to write it. *Sarafina!* turned out to be Ngema's greatest hit yet: its initial ten-week engagement at Lincoln Center was extended numerous times before the show moved to the Cort Theatre on Broadway, where it played to full houses for a year and a half; then it toured the United States, and a second company was formed to tour Europe and Japan.

Meanwhile, back in 1986, Duma Ndlovu, a South African writer and producer then living in New York in exile, who was critically involved in bringing Ngema's work to Lincoln Center, asked me if I would think about writing a book with him concerning black South African theater, with special emphasis on Ngema. Having great enthusiasm for Ngema as an artist and as a person, I didn't have to think long, although it took us some years to get started. Then in 1990, just when we'd begun our collaboration, Ndlovu found a way to return permanently to South Africa, and he decided to move on to a new life and new projects in the land of his birth. He left the book project behind as a kind of gift to me.

What I've written on my own is not a survey of South African theater, as we originally planned, but the story of Mbongeni Ngema, in the telling of which I've tried to incorporate information about the country and its theater as it lies within the sweep of the narrative. I've based this material on uncountable hours of interviews with Ngema and on the oral testimony of people who have known him—his family and friends; his former lovers and present wives; promoters, mentors, professional adversaries—which I collected during two extended trips to South Africa, in 1990 and 1991. The bulk of the book was written well before the 1994 elections.

Ngema took me everywhere I wanted to go in South Africa when we were in the country at the same time; he told me stories full of vitality and subtlety, and he never once paused before answering any question. The people I interviewed, whether they were Ngema's friends and family or were at odds with him, were almost always unhesitatingly forthcoming with their accounts. Most of them, seeing that I was a young woman traveling alone and far from home, treated me as a daughter or a sister in need of guardianship.

After completing the manuscript, I again returned to South Africa—Ngema, feeling that he wanted some help with his newest musical, had invited me to write it with him. During the first six months of 1993, when I worked with the company of our play and stayed with them in a Johannesburg hotel, my relationship with Ngema and his theater and with South Africa became far more personal than it had been during the writing of Ngema's story. In an epilogue, I have described this latest experience with a tone that differs somewhat from the preceding chapters. When I wrote it, I had just returned from Africa where I had actually had a hand in releasing some of that fierce joy I had observed as an outsider, back in the eighties in Harlem. For me, many things would never be the same. I don't think, however, that the principal effect of my new intimacy with Ngema's theater was partiality; if anything, it demystified his creative process and allowed me to witness, firsthand, many forceful aspects of his character that I'd only previously inferred from rumor or from his own descriptions of himself. Most importantly, through this experience, I was allowed an opportunity to live in South Africa, for a while, as an insider.

One hopes for the best for South Africa, that at least things won't get worse, and that long-patient souls won't be strained beyond their limits. Americans who ask me how I like South Africa usually seem surprised and somewhat disapproving when I tell them that I have loved being there. In the cities, I've encountered paranoia and distrust, ugly scenes and some repulsive racists. But it is reassuring to remember that in the homes and theaters of most of the people I've had occasion to visit, I've found the most generous hospitality imaginable and a wealth of resilient love.

A section of photographs appears between pages 82 and 83.

ACKNOWLEDGMENTS

▼

Without a loving family and true friends in America—Phyllis and Henry Cretors, Fred and LuAnn Jones, Karin Barry, Jacqueline de la Chaume, Jenny Gersten, Margot Guralnick, Elaine Moore, Christopher Randolph, Andrea Scott, and Mason Wiley—I would never have gotten to Africa. Other indispensable support and advice came from David Stanford, Elizabeth Kaplan, Risa Schwartz, Warren Beatty, Larry Sloan, Perry Lang, John Guare, Dumisane Mtimkulu, Renata Miller and the Writers Room, Steven Gaydos, Cathy Barnett, Voza Rivers, Ricardo Khan and Crossroads Theatre, and everyone at Lincoln Center Theater.

During my first visits to South Africa, Mannie Manim, Barney Simon, John Kani, and their staff at the Market Theatre were enormously helpful; later, Michal Grobbelaar, Alan Joseph, and their associates at the Civic Theatre were the perfect hosts. Thanks also to Mark Rosin, of Jacobson, Rosin & Wright, Jenny Garson, Bheki Khoza, Maishe Maponya, and Matsemela Manaka.

Duma Ndlovu introduced me to Mbongeni Ngema and persuaded me to write about him in spite of my self-doubts. I was guided through South Africa by numerous members of Ngema's extended clan of family and friends, most of whom I've named in this book. (If they're public figures or have ever been listed in a program or playbill, I've referenced them by both first and last name. To protect their anonymity, I've identified those individuals who have avoided the limelight—people struggling to live a natural life in South Africa—by first name only.) *Ngiyabonga.*

NOTHING
EXCEPT OURSELVES

INTRODUCTION

▼

There's nothing neat and tidy about me, like a nice social revolution. With me goes a mad, passionate, insane, screaming world of ten thousand devils, and the man who lifts the lid off this suppressed world does so at his peril.
                                                    BESSIE HEAD[1]

At the age of thirty-nine, Mbongeni Ngema has already lived a long life. It began in Natal province, near Durban, where he was born in 1955, seven years after Hendrik Verwoerd coined the term *apartheid.* Almost every year since then, until very recently, new or revised pieces of legislation were introduced to limit or squelch the potential in black people like Ngema. For much of his youth he was virtually homeless and dreamless. On his own, in pursuit of a high school education, he zigzagged through rural Zululand and the urban ghettos near Durban, sponging off any obscure acquaintance or distant relative who would have him. Later, hoping to stumble into a job in the overpeopled migrant labor force, he drifted from one cold, massive factory to another.

Then, as a young adult, he saw his first play and became stagestruck. Homeless still, he gathered a band of amateur actors and rehearsed a musical—about an infamous serial killer—in backyards in black townships, and slept on floors in houses belonging to people he'd just met. He traveled across the Drakensberg escarpment to Soweto to find Gibson Kente, "the father of South African theater." He wended his way to the Transkei, where he was thrown into a solitary prison cell simply because he'd written a play. But not long after, he found himself at the preeminent theaters and awards ceremonies of America and Europe. And in 1990, a few days after Nelson Mandela was released from prison, Ngema snubbed the apartheid law by moving into an elegant ranch-style house with a swimming pool and a tennis court in a suburb of Johannesburg that was officially designated white, where jacarandas bloomed above the cares and politics of men. The odds against someone with Ngema's background arriving at such a destiny—the numbers may vary, depending on whose population statistics you believe—are roughly 30 million to one. The chances that a black man will discover his own unique talents in the course of a typically disquieting life in that country are slim; that he might triumph in a domain as rarefied as the international theater has been, till now, unimaginable.

There has been little written about black South African theater. The only playscripts published recently in America, besides the work of the white dramatist Athol Fugard, are in an anthology Duma Ndlovu edited, called *Woza Afrika*. And a book entitled *South African People's Plays*, published in London in 1981, featured the best examples of politically oriented "black" theater up to 1976. It should be no surprise that behind each playwright's name on the latter volume's table of contents lies a troubling story of talent or destiny confounded:

Gibson Kente, a man who plays an important role in Ngema's story, was once the most popular and successful director-producer in the black townships nationwide, but at a certain point in his career, shortly after he was detained as an enemy of the state for writing material deemed subversive, he began to express some unmistakably reactionary ideas through his plays. On more than one occasion, his house in Soweto has been firebombed by the young "comrades" who, after the student uprisings of 1976, assumed absolute reign over the urban township citizenry. Nevertheless, he has survived each attack, continues his theater work, and pursues his unpopular, conservative ideas.

Credo V. Mutwa derived his play *uNosilimela* from the traditional African legends and folklore to which most people in the detribalized urban centers had lost their connection and which Steve Biko and other Black Consciousness leaders stressed the importance of rediscovering. But in 1976, Mutwa reportedly wrote a traitorous letter to the minister of justice, Jimmy Kruger, in which he compared Biko's

Black Consciousness movement to Nazism and implored the government to call in its full military force to quash the Soweto rioters. Although he denied making the statements when they appeared in the newspapers, his outraged neighbors burned his Soweto house to the ground. Later, he found refuge with the Soweto Parks and Recreation Department, went on the public payroll, and lived behind a high security fence. Today, he practices as a *Sangoma*—a healer and a fortune teller.

Mthuli Shezi's only play, *Shanti,* still stands as a stimulus and inspiration for politically motivated writers, although it was never performed in the author's lifetime. On a train platform one day shortly after completing his script, he saw that white railroad employees were harassing some black women. He stood up to the men and defended the women. In the same location on a day soon afterward, the same men spotted Shezi and punished him for his brazenness by pushing him onto the rails before an oncoming train.

Steve Biko wrote that "one escapes all these possible areas of pitfalls where one might die without any explanation. It is not because you are well kept, it is not because you are well protected, it is just a miracle, it happens."[2]

In 1913, the introduction of the draconian Natives Land Act instantly created what the South African writer Bessie Head has described as "a floating, landless proletariat whose labor could be used and manipulated at will." This legislation made it illegal for "Africans" to own land in all but the 6 percent of the country designated as tribal reserves or "homelands"; in subsequent years, the land allocation was increased to 13 percent, and by the time the law was repealed, in 1991, Africans constituted roughly 75 percent of the total population. They were considered only temporary residents in the towns where they migrated to work, they had virtually no legal recourse, and so many laws were created to limit their rights that they could never be sure at any moment that they weren't committing a criminal act. "We don't know where we are running to except that we must run," Ms. Head wrote.

Ngema's early life was typical in this respect: he was always running away from some danger, some calamity. But at a certain point in his young adulthood, and with little ado about the conversion, he sud-

3

denly realized that he could run *toward* a destination. That unhesitating about-face was the most important move in his life. Throughout the better part of this century, it has been utterly impractical for a black person in South Africa to set any goals at all for himself regardless of his talents or of his will. Were it not for some unlikely, unpredictable twists of fate, Ngema might never have become an exception; he might well be working today in a factory, or be in prison, or be dead.

He gives large credit for his survival to *amadlozi,* his ancestors, to whom he regularly prays and pays tribute, and to those living people who sheltered and championed him throughout the early, errant years of his life—his many friends and his infinitely extending family. By South African tradition, Ngema is a "brother" not only to the other offspring of his father and mother and to all of his first cousins but to every Ngema in the land, whether or not there is a traceable family connection. Relatives of his parents' generation are fathers and mothers to Ngema. Furthermore, tied to Ngema are a number of clan-names—Madlokovu, Nene, Mngadi, Sithenjwa. Linked to Ngema's mother's family, the Hadebes, is another litany of clans. Ngema may not marry any woman who, as a member of this wide-ranging sphere, would be considered his sister. An actual feeling of intimate brotherhood exists between Ngema and those relatives whom Westerners would regard as cousins. And just as no brother, however distantly related, ever turned Ngema away from his house in the early days, Ngema has now enveloped scores of his kin into his theater company and true home—Committed Artists.

Ngema's major plays have all arisen from outrage at circumstances created by politicians and tyrants. But although in the brutal conflict between the African National Congress and the Inkatha Freedom Party he came down squarely on the side of the ANC, Ngema has never officially joined a political party. His only unconditionally binding ties are to his vast family, to the memory and the land of his ancestors, to himself, and to his work as an artist. Today, having written a few plays about some of the events shaking South Africa in his own lifetime, the stories that seem to inspire him most deeply are the ones that have been around the longest—the stories of the famous African wars, featuring kings and soldiers with names such as Cetshwayo, Bambatha, Cijimpi.

Ngema has often been a subject of heated discussion and debate. Based on legitimate revolutionary principles, some black separatists and other dogmatists have denounced him for living among white people, working with white-run theaters, and converting "the people's struggle" into commercial hits. His plays *Woza Albert!*, *Asinamali!*, and *Sarafina!* actually aroused little controversy; but a later play, *Township Fever*, which was based on a momentous workers' strike directed by the ANC-affiliated union federation, Cosatu, created something of a firestorm.

There are also rumors of a casting couch at Committed Artists and censure for Ngema's well-publicized polygamy—the preparations for his 1991 wedding to his second (concurrent) wife were covered for weeks in the press. Some theater workers disdain his practice of casting youngsters, whom he thoroughly trains and commands as a sort of patriarch, when there are so many professional actors around, wallowing in unemployment. Many of these arguments are valid. There are also, as in every artistic community, people whose critical opinions are based solely on personal jealousies and rivalries.

But all these considerations stand apart from Ngema's talent. Few would deny that he has enormous creative gifts. Most black South Africans recognize themselves in his highly entertaining plays; they derive deep pleasure from his music and a feeling of pride from his personal success. In fact, Ngema's achievement has been a result of their shared pride. By inviting the struggling young Mbongeni Ngema and his partners to sleep on their floors, eat at their tables, and share their paychecks and savings, black South Africans voluntarily taxed themselves to support the success of one of their own.

In 1990, when two companies of *Sarafina!* were running simultaneously, in Europe and America, actors and musicians were making wages never dreamed of among black South Africans. Whenever Ngema announces auditions, hundreds of youngsters spend their only pennies on one-way train tickets from Cape Town, the northern Transvaal, and KwaZulu to Johannesburg, where, more often than not, they don't know a soul. After tryouts for the second company of

Sarafina!, Ngema had to hire taxis to deliver scores of the unchosen back to their remote homes. Ngema has the power now to miraculously transform their lives as his life was once transformed—largely because of his own extraordinary drive and talents, but also because black society willed him to succeed. His story tells not just of one man's rise but of how a people who were in every way oppressed chose to create among them an artist in their own image.

Chapter One

▼

*To be born is to come into the world weighed down with strange gifts of the
soul, with enigmas and an inextinguishable sense of exile. So it was with me.*
                                        BEN OKRI,
                                        The Famished Road[1]

Mbongeni Ngema's paternal grandfather, Vukayibambe, was born in
1872, seven years before the Zulu forces were defeated by the British
at the battle of Ulundi, and he lived to the age of 116. Most of the traditional cultural and military systems survived European dominance
intact well into Vukayibambe's adulthood. Like his male ancestors, he
was bound to serve in a reserve regiment of the Zulu king's army until
the best of his fighting days were over. Although as a young man he
was granted leave to work for his livelihood in the then British-
administered national police force, he was forbidden by custom to
marry until middle age, when he was permanently released from his
military obligation. Consequently, he was fifty years old before the
birth of his first child, a son whom he named Zwelikhethabantu.

Vukayibambe became a policeman in the late nineteenth century,
when Johannesburg was a skeletal gold-rush town with little more than
a post office, a train depot, and a police station to foreshadow the sophisticated city that was germinating there. He was often commissioned to escort black criminals from Johannesburg to a prison in
Eshowe in Natal province, where he was based, six hundred kilome-
ters on foot. Later in life, he would entertain his children by telling

them how his prisoners, if they were wily, could prolong the journey and delay their imprisonment: When night fell, and the men lay down to sleep in the open air, Vukayibambe would place his spear on the ground with the iron tip pointed like the needle of a compass toward Natal; if his wards managed to rotate it a little to the left while he slept, in the morning he would unsuspectingly lead them to Swaziland. He fell for the deception more than once.

Zwelikhethabantu was a young man when he joined Vukayibambe at the Eshowe police station, not far from their ancestral home in Hlabisa. Together, aged father and young son conducted official expeditions through the mountainous terrain of northeastern Zululand. In the course of these journeys Zwelikhethabantu came to know and love a young girl named Gladys Hadebe, who lived with her family in the village of Nyoni, just north of where the Tugela River flows into the Indian Ocean. The couple had their first child, a son named Johannes, before Gladys reached her teens. Eight years later, around the time of birth of their second son, Mandla, they married and moved to Verulam, a minor coastal city with a large Indian population an hour north of Durban, where the Pretoria-based police bureaucracy, now an Afrikaner club, had transferred Zwelikhethabantu.

Mbongeni Ngema was born in Verulam on June 1, 1955, the third of seven children. He came into the world with his tiny, fragile hands clenched in fists that could not be unlocked. His bones were weak, and he was a sickly child. Zwelikhethabantu was a prominent member of the conservative Shembe Nazareth Baptist Church and highly regarded by its prophet, Johannes Galilee, to whom he turned for the healing of his son. He knew well that medicine of any kind—Western as well as traditional African—was considered taboo by the church, so Zwelikhethabantu was shocked when the prophet instructed him to take the baby, then three months old, for treatment at McCords Hospital in Durban. There, after a long period of illness, the child finally gained his strength, and his hands unfolded.

The prophet said that the hands had been clutching a gift that Ngema had carried with him into this world, and he developed a special fondness for the child. Every Saturday, thousands of worshipers in billowing white robes congregated on a vast, sweeping hill at the site of the main church in Inanda for a day-long service. Before beginning his sermon, Johannes Galilee would often call into his microphone: "Mr. Ngema, bring my son to me." Zwelikhethabantu would carry Mbongeni through the crowds and place him on the prophet's lap; then the service could begin.

The Shembe Nazareth Church is one of the largest and most conservative of many Zionist sects rooted in black communities across South Africa, which synthesize indigenous African beliefs with extrinsic Christian doctrine. Saturday is their day of pious devotion; the faithful wear white robes for a somber ceremony and eschew hot food and hot drink.

Every Sunday, the day appointed for feasting and celebration, the Ngema family would return to the same hill in festive traditional costumes. Divided into groups according to sex, age, and marital status, the parishioners would perform the tribal songs and dances beneath the open sky, where their prayers might be best heard by the ancestors, simultaneously fulfilling the call of Psalms to "let the hills be joyful together before the Lord." While the conventions of European drama and spectacle existed completely outside of Ngema's orbit, he was exposed from the earliest possible age to a form of theater directly related to the dramatic enactments presented at the courts of the great Zulu kings before the undoing of the sovereignty—a pageantry both solemn and joyous, in which he took part every weekend until he was ten years old.

▼

Before 1953, when Hendrik Verwoerd entered a new act called Bantu Education into the apartheid lawbooks, the South African government did not provide schools for African children. Only those who lived close to institutions established by Christian missionaries received a formal— and free—education. After the introduction of Bantu Education, a far greater number of children had access to schools, but their attendance was not mandatory, and they had to pay for the privilege. And while the generally liberal aim of the missionaries had been to assimilate their black students into European society, the new government-prescribed syllabus was designed to train them to be servants someday to the white children seated at neat desks in well-appointed classrooms in a separate system that was far superior, mandatory, and tuition-free.

Fees, books, and uniforms were so costly, relative to wages, that few black parents could afford to keep all of their children enrolled regularly. During the ensuing years, political unrest, police detention, and family crises also impeded dedicated study, as they continue to do in present times. In 1991, only 10 percent of African high school matriculants qualified for university admission, and in the entire country, only nineteen African high school seniors graduated with an A average.[2]

Because Zwelikhethabantu earned a slightly above-average wage, he was able, with some creative industry on the side, to keep his children in school in those early years. In time, by studying and passing a series of government exams, he made his way up through the ranks to become chief sergeant—the highest position attainable by a black officer. It is a matter of pride in the Ngema family that he never made an arrest—except for one celebrated capture, of which more later. According to the family legend, if, for example, another officer brought someone in on a passbook offense—which meant that the domestic passport all adult Africans were required to carry to attest to their legal, residential, employment, and tax-payment status was somehow out of order or missing a stamp or notation—Zwelikhethabantu would wait until the station was empty and say to the prisoner, "Why haven't you paid your taxes? Go. Run, right now. If they catch you again, I'm going to have to lock you inside."

He had no power to impress the law upon the white or Indian citizens of Verulam, but he was beloved by the black citizens over whom he did have jurisdiction. Because of the antagonistic complexity of the apartheid laws—the entire canon of racial law pertaining only to Africans, before the present era of reformation, weighed well over ten pounds[3]—most of them, at one time or another, or many times, found themselves before him.

Among his fellow black policemen, however, Zwelikhethabantu was a mildly controversial figure. Strict bureaucratic codes requiring all officers to come to work neatly groomed conflicted with the rules of his church, which forbade him to cut his hair. He appealed to police headquarters in Pretoria and was granted a rare dispensation to wear his hair and his beard distinctively long. He stood out strikingly among his co-workers, many of whom begrudged him his privilege, but Zwelikhethabantu was above petty rivalry, and he was content.

This was well before leaders of the Black Consciousness movement began to advance an attitude of hostility toward black policemen. In 1971, Steve Biko said that "there is no such thing as a black policeman. Any black man who props the system up actively has lost the right to being considered part of the black world."[4] But in the late 1950s, that he might be a prop or a puppet of the apartheid system—even if he refused to arrest anybody—would not have occurred to Zwelikhethabantu. He felt fortunate to be considered an honorable cop and a responsible parent, and to have achieved a relatively high position in one of the few professions offering a nearly decent wage to black men. He could afford to send all his children to school and to support them in a few of their extracurricular interests as well. When he detected a musical gift in his oldest son, Johannes, he bought him a guitar.

Zwelikhethabantu was obliged to comply with four distinct and rigid codes of behavior—those dictated by his employer, the chief of police; by the church; by the discriminatory apartheid regime; and by his Zulu forebears—which necessitated superhuman self-restraint and composure on his part. The tolerance and compassion that he applied to his work he applied at home too, and although he was tendered the bashful respect he commanded as a Zulu patriarch, he rarely disciplined the children and was well loved by them. Ngema's mother, Ma Hadebe (after a woman marries, she becomes known by her maiden name), was still a young slip of a woman, but she was the hot-handed disciplinarian in the family. She was also a shrewd entrepreneur and found numerous ways to supplement the family income. She bought knitting machines and put both Ngema and his older brother Mandla to work making sweaters, which she sold to local women. She took her daughter Fikile to Durban to buy discounted clothes, which they peddled in Verulam for a small profit. She kept careful accounts of the household funds and made precise budgets. She sometimes beat the children badly when they misbehaved, and she held them in a constant state of frightened submission, but in this manner, she was able to keep the family unified in their goals and in their four-room house—for a while.

When their work was finished, the children were encouraged to explore their talents. With his father's endorsement, Johannes formed a musical group called The Waves and performed at private parties and in church halls. Ngema was only a preschooler at the time, but he stayed close to Johannes and learned how to hold and strum the guitar and, soon, to play the Beatles songs his brother's band featured. Ngema made his own guitar from a discarded tin can and some string, and performed on a street corner for pennies.

Ma Hadebe's sister Joyce, whom the family calls *Mama omncane* (little mama) because she is the youngest sister, lived nearby and frequently took Ngema to the *stokvels,* where the young boy would sing and dance to entertain the crowd for small change. It was a time of prohibition, enforced upon the African populace only, but people in the townships could drink bootleg and homemade liquor at shebeens—illicit taverns like juke joints—set up in private homes, subject to police raids and graft, and at private parties hosted by rotating members of *stokvels,* neighborhood money-making associations. The host would supply music—e.g., little Mbongeni Ngema—and refreshments, which he would sell or auction for personal profit at grossly inflated prices. Such parties usually attracted a crush of friends and neighbors, who gladly paid for the entertainment. They knew that the next event might be their own and that they would have their turn to profit. But a large part of the appeal, aside from the conviviality of the affair, was the vicarious pleasure derived from watching the host's earnings grow.

Because family reunions were important to Zwelikhethabantu, he took Ma Hadebe and the children to the ancestral farm in Hlabisa—more specifically in eNhlwathi, one of numerous tribally administered districts, or *izigodi,* within the area of Hlabisa—whenever there was a feast or wedding. Vukayibambe had retired from the police force, but he was still vigorous and active. He was the patriarch of a large extended family and, as district *induna* (headman), a position of great honor, presided over the tribal law council. He lived with his ancient mother and his three wives, each in her own hut, and uncountable children on a vast piece of land that the family still occupies and cultivates today, though it has greatly diminished over the years and no longer yields a sustaining crop. In Zulu custom, land belongs not to any individual but to the entire tribe. As relatives were displaced from their urban communities through government-enforced removals or deported on pass-law violations out of the cities and into the homelands—where their families might not have lived for generations—every acre gradually filled up. Under the Natives Land Act of 1913, the most fertile parcels of land in the Zulu domain were given to white farmers and declared South African territory. Patched in between remained seventy major and minor fragments of the least desirable land, designated as the KwaZulu homeland (aka Zululand). Today less than 20 percent of KwaZulu is arable and more than 80 percent of the country's rural homeland residents live below the poverty line.[5]

During Ngema's childhood, however, the farm in Hlabisa still throve and abundantly fed the large family that lived there in a settlement of mud rondavels. There were fields of corn, cotton, pumpkins, and beans, a great multitude of cows, and an army of children to tend it all. Since the occasions that drew him to Hlabisa were usually festive, Ngema enjoyed these visits. For his entertainment there were well-rehearsed dances performed to the music of a penny whistle, the irrepressible voices of young girls, and the thump of a plastic drum. In a segregated area within a bramble enclosure, the men would eat the best parts of the beast that had been slaughtered to honor the ancestors, sing, and outdo each other with their high-kicking dances. Ngema and the other boys would play games, duel with sticks, and watch their elders from the periphery of the adult activity. The cousins who lived in eNhlwathi year-round had arduous responsibilities on the farm, but Ngema had none and could love the country unconditionally. The children were always the last to be fed and received the least delectable portions of meat, but when there is more than enough, this is not such a hardship.

At night, by candlelight, Vukayibambe would tell long, intricately woven tales that he liked to abandon at the point of greatest suspense. Ngema's great-grandmother still had vivid memories of the Zulu-British war of 1879—of King Cetshwayo's triumph at Isandhlwana and his downfall at Ulundi. She told stories of the Zulu warriors who took refuge in a cave in eNhlwathi Mountain during some of the most famous battles, many of which were decided within sight of the Ngema homestead. Before the Zulu devastation, her husband Cijimpi, a captain of that war, had not been unique among the regiments in his sustaining faith in the invincibility of the great Zulu army. He survived the brutal defeat at Ulundi, but not his disillusionment and his shame. As he entered the family kraal upon his return from combat, he fell limply to the ground, ostensibly dying of heartbreak.

In Ngema's time, as it did in Cijimpi's, and as it does today, the Zulu nightfall radically extinguished the brilliant cheer of the day. The night was very long and blindingly dark when the moon was not full. The silence was vivid, underscored by the vibrations of insects, broken only by the stray moans of cows. Storytelling helped to shorten and brighten the night and to lighten the loneliness it heaped on a person.

▼

Although he was kept rigorously occupied, Ngema remembers the first ten years of his life as a happy time. He did well in school, and by 1966—when everything changed—he had passed successfully through Standard Two, roughly equivalent to the American fourth grade.

Urban segregation, like racism, was the de facto law of South Africa long before the invention of apartheid in 1948 and the Group Areas Act of 1950, which strictly decreed that Whites, Asians, Coloreds, and Africans outside the tribal reserves were to live in circumscribed communities among their own kind—in the fulfillment of which more than 3.5 million black South Africans were uprooted and relocated against their will. But when Ngema was a child, there were still some places, like Verulam, where whites, blacks, and Indians could at least live in proximity, if not in neighborliness or parity. Zwelikhethabantu had the use of a neat four-room house in a peaceful section of town near the police station and the privilege of raising his children in a way that was natural and rewarding to him. For the children, life moved with the steady, upward-climbing slowness of ordinary childhood, until 1966, when the government designated Verulam as an Indians-only community under the Group Areas Act, and hastened their transition into adulthood.

Zwelikhethabantu was informed that while he could keep his job, he would have to relinquish his house. Because of his respected position, he was permitted to make his own arrangements for the move. But other black families in Verulam were forced out by soldiers, who came in trucks to transport them to KwaMashu, an Africans-only township that had been built nearby.

Ma Hadebe and Zwelikhethabantu were provided with lodgings in a barracks in town but no longer had a place for the children, so they sent them to live with their grandfather in Hlabisa. For Ngema, life changed drastically for the next four years. Each morning, he rose with the other children at two o'clock to harness a span of oxen and drive them down to till the fields by the light of a lantern. He'd finish there by six, make the forty-five-minute walk back home, bathe, dress in his school uniform, eat *amasi* (curdled milk), and walk to school. At three in the afternoon, when class was dismissed, he'd run home, terrified of keeping his grandfather waiting, quickly eat some cornmeal porridge, and run down to the fields where the herd was grazing. The cows knew their own schedule well; by five o'clock they would be preparing themselves to return to the kraal, and by seven o'clock the final stragglers in the long procession would be safely inside for the night. Ngema would eat a little more, prepare for bed, and fall asleep by nine. There weren't enough hours in the day for homework.

Vukayibambe kept more than five hundred head of cattle on his farm and had, by all accounts, a profound love for each one individually. He knew them by their physical markings and their temperaments, and he imparted this familiarity and appreciation to his children and grandchildren. As the herd returned from the fields, he would stand at the entrance to the homestead, an imposing, white-bearded figure, holding a tall wooden staff, and sing ecstatic praises to each cow. The cattle responded with emphatic moos, nods, and snorts; some of them seemed to love the singing—to love the *man*—so much that they would stop and wait until he'd finished a song before they'd pass him. Like Vukayibambe's early treks from Johannesburg to

Eshowe, the daily migrations of his cattle, from the pasture to the kraal, were usually prolonged, lingering affairs.

In addition to this herd, Vukayibambe owned cattle all over Zululand, on loan to needy families who used them for milk and hoped that they'd multiply. If the original cows were never returned, it was not of much consequence to Vukayibambe, because he had plenty. He was a rich man in the multitude and affection of his beasts.

Looking back now, Ngema is grateful for the enlarging experience of his years on the farm, and his unconditional love for the land has been restored. But he hated it at the time, especially the waking in the forsaking dark. Like all boys in his world, he learned at an early age that a man should never cry. But he was still a young child, far from his mother, and wretchedly lonely for her. At the end of 1967, when his father was transferred to Mtubatuba, which was considerably closer than Verulam, he began to see more of his parents. His daily drill remained the same, however, and didn't let up until he finished Standard Six, the highest level of study offered at the local school. Then he was sent away. In the remaining years of his education, he would be relocated repeatedly, and it would be a long time—not until he was an adult with some success in the theater—before he would enjoy a sense of home again.

▼

His parents sent him back to the Verulam area to stay with his brother Johannes, who was living with a girlfriend and her family in a black township near a high school. Soon Mandla, who had applied for a post as a policeman and was told that he would receive a commission at any moment, joined them. But the arrangement lasted only a short time; Johannes and his girlfriend began to fight, and soon their relationship ended.

Ngema and Mandla found temporary refuge in a squatter camp nearby, a dangerous area, with an excess of misery, drunkenness, and violent crime. The low-built shanty they shared with some friends was unbearably crowded. Tangled bodies struggled for sleep on the ground, beneath an unattached roof. The school was an arduous bus ride away, and the bedlam at home was disturbing Ngema's studies, so he and Mandla decided to leave and to become, like David Copperfield, the heroes of their own lives.

In the center of Verulam was an expansive dairy farm owned by an Englishman named Beckett and superintended by an old man named Shandu, a friend of their father's from church. Shandu lived on the property in a shack too tiny to accommodate guests. But the Ngema boys knew the farm very well from their early days in Verulam, when they frequently played there, and they devised a system that allowed them to live there in secret.

Each night they lingered in town until it became very dark; then they jumped the fence and headed to Beckett's stable—which was well heated by the cows—and slept beneath a blanket of straw. They kept a cloth and a comb at an unused tap, where they washed every morning. While Ngema was in school, Mandla waited in town for news of his appointment.

Once a week during the four months they camped on the farm, Shandu would invite them for a meal of *amasi*. Each time, a moment would come when the old man lowered his voice and said, as Ngema and Mandla froze in dread: "There is something going on. Every night the dogs are barking, and they never bark for nothing."

"Yes, father?" the boys would say.

"But the gate is so far away from where I sleep that the thieves are always gone by the time I get there. Strange, but they haven't stolen anything yet."

For other meals they were largely dependent on Mandla's girlfriend, who lived in KwaMashu and had a little money. She frequently slept with them in the stable. On the weekends she would take their dirty clothes home with her, wash and iron them, and occasionally return with enough cash to treat them to a meal at an Indian restaurant. The boys, always voracious, would order greedily. One time when the waiter brought the check, the girlfriend reached into her pocket and found it empty. She emptied her shoes, shook her clothing, but she couldn't find the money. And the proprietor called the police. Although it was fortunate that the officer who responded was a friend of their father's and, rather than hauling them away, did them the favor of paying the bill, it was precisely the kind of encounter they'd been trying to avoid.

Zwelikhethabantu believed that Ngema and Mandla were still living with Johannes's girlfriend. He would have objected strenuously to their illicit residence in Beckett's stable; he might very well have ordered them back to Hlabisa, where they would have to devote themselves entirely to the farm, a prospect the boys shuddered at and would do their best to escape. Occasionally they had to go to the police station to retrieve money their father had sent there for them, but most of the time they were particularly careful to avoid the police and anyone else who knew their father and might contact him to tell him what they were up to. These precautions and the reassurance they derived from their constant companionship made it possible for them to uphold their independent lifestyle for many months—until Mandla received word that he had been appointed to a police station in Krugersdorp, near Johannesburg. And his departure left Ngema, only fourteen years old, utterly alone.

The pitch-black nights in the cowshed became lonely and terrifying. For company after school, Ngema began to associate with gangs of rough youths, who introduced him to liquor—cheap wine in jumbo-size bottles. On the weekends, he would join his new friends at the train station, where they would panhandle and offer themselves as porters. At night, in the dark, he climbed the fence alone, tore to the cowshed as Shandu's dogs howled and bayed, buried himself in his bed of straw, and tried to sleep.

▼

Ngema's parents decided that he should spend the next year earning money to pay future school fees and to buy himself some new clothes. They soon relocated him to Mtubatuba, where his mother had found a job for him. Zwelikhethabantu had been transferred again, this time to Tugela Ferry, the seat of a district of rural slums on the western border of Natal, as part of a special unit commissioned to subdue the brutal faction fighting that had been raging there among the local *izigodi* for many generations. In the beginning of their conflict, the men of this region employed spears and clubs to kill each other; in later years, they built blunderbusses; by the time Zwelikhethabantu arrived to intercede, they had acquired South African–made automatic rifles and Soviet AK-47s. He slept with Ma Hadebe—who firmly believed that her husband couldn't take care of himself and had resolved to accompany him wherever he went—in a tent pitched on a bank of the Tugela River.

Ma Hadebe heard that the government was building a new township at Mtubatuba, and she sent Ngema to live with a dear friend in the area—an old woman who alone cared for four young daughters—while he worked as an apprentice to a team of bricklayers. He earned 25 rand a month for helping to build as many as ten four-room houses a week. Every night he'd fall into bed, white with cement, feeling as if he'd been beaten. When he arose in the morning, he felt he'd slept only an hour, and he returned to the construction site with his young body cramped and sore.

The old mama was miserably poor, but she took Ngema into her home and treated him like a son. In the beginning, she appreciated his polite manners and enjoyed the music he was always playing on the guitar that had become his constant companion. When he entered into a shy, chaste romance with one of her daughters—when they parted company, they showed their love by throwing pebbles at each other—she was delighted. But it wasn't long before Ngema's charm began to wear thin.

At the end of each month the construction workers would clean themselves up, pile into the back of a flatbed truck, and head to the government offices in town to receive their pay. Waiting outside the building were the women who had been selling them food and sorghum beer all month on credit. By the time Ngema settled his debts, he had nothing left to offer his hostess. Month after month he came home with the same excuse, gradually draining her affection for him. When the year was over, he found that he had sown some discontent, helped to build hundreds of matchbook houses, and learned something about bricklaying, but he hadn't saved a cent.

Ma Hadebe determined to get him back in school. She wrote a letter to another friend in the Verulam area, a woman with a large family in a four-room house, and arranged for Ngema to stay with them while he attended his old school again.

There were many beautiful girls in this family, and Ngema fell hard for one of them, a twenty-six-year-old woman who introduced him to the pleasures of adult love. Ngema slept in a bedroom with the boys. During the week, when her father stayed in a work hostel, Ngema's sweetheart shared her mother's bed in the master bedroom. But on the weekends, when the father came home from the hostel to sleep with his wife, the sweetheart bedded down on the floor of the dining room among her many sisters. It was then that Ngema could be with her. He would wait for the household to fall asleep and quietly go to her. In the early morning, he'd return to his room before the father stirred.

One weekend, while he was waiting for the house to settle into a safe silence, Ngema dropped off himself, and woke in a panic just before dawn. Because he was desperate to be with his lover, he took a dangerous chance. He slipped out of his room, into the dining room, and beneath her blanket. He embraced her. Then, abruptly, he was disturbed by the light of a kerosene lamp and the sound of heavy footsteps. He clung to the woman tightly, buried his head beneath the blanket, and held his breath.

The footsteps approached, and when they came to a halt, Ngema heard from above the tremulous voice of the father: "My daughter, who is that on top of you?" Ngema recoiled from his lover, dashed for the boys' bedroom, fled through the window, and ran for several hours to the home of an aunt in another, distant township, never to return.

For the next two years, he drifted about the Durban-area townships, staying with a series of obscure friends and relatives. He settled for a while in Umlazi, the largest black township of Natal, with the Gumedes, the family of *Mama omncane's* lover. At Vukuzakhe High School, he favored history and read the English textbooks as if they were novels—he ignored the fact that, written from a European point of view, they omitted the African war stories he loved best. He was by nature a good student, but outside distractions had begun to overwhelm his interest. He would sometimes disappear from class for as long as two months at a time, returning just to take exams. He managed to pass Standards Eight and Nine in this manner, but he came to be regarded by his teachers as a problem child—a brilliant but derelict student.

He'd fallen in love again, with a girl named Monica, who was foremost among his diversions. (He would stay involved with her, sporadically, for many years; though they never married, they eventually had a son named Afrika, Ngema's only child.) In those days, schoolmasters were very strict and frequently resorted to corporal punishments. Because romance was virtually outlawed on school grounds, most students hid their affairs as a matter of course. But Ngema and Monica flaunted their love, holding hands in the hallways and brazenly exhibiting their affection, and thus deepened the dismay of their teachers.

Ngema was also singing and playing guitar with a band in the nearby township of Clermont, which exhausted what remained of his time and energy. He infuriated a once-sympathetic vice-principal, who had taken a special interest in his case and tried many tricks to lure him into regular attendance—he entered him in a school-wide English competition (Ngema won it without studying) and collected funds from the student body to buy instruments for a school band, which he hoped would keep the errant student on the premises. Despite the vice-principal's efforts, Ngema dropped out at the beginning of his final year. He had high hopes for the Clermont band and moved in with his fellow musicians for a while. But when the band broke up, he soon found himself homeless again and retreated to Hlabisa, putting his education decisively behind him.

Ngema knew that he was Zwelikhethabantu's favorite son, the one on whom he'd pinned his highest hopes. He expected his father's disappointment and his mother's fury, but because he had advanced further in the educational system than most children did, he hoped their displeasure would quickly diminish. In fact, far graver matters soon demanded their concern. Perhaps under the stress and anguish of his post in Tugela Ferry, Zwelikhethabantu's health had begun to deteriorate. He requested a transfer and returned home to Hlabisa, where he shortly suffered a critical stroke that left him immobile and severely impaired his speech for the rest of his life.

Zwelikhethabantu lived for eight more years, but for Ngema, his father's stroke and the end of his own schooling meant the effective end of his childhood. Now he would have to face problems that had seemed remote when he was in school. There a young girl had loved him and a principal had seen potential in him, giving him a stimulating sense of his own distinction and talents. In the next few years he would have to work; in the world he was about to enter, he would find few champions. His interests were boundless—music, sports, history, love—but his career options were dishearteningly finite. As he and his family saw it, he could join the migratory laborers seeking employment in the factories and the mines, or he could, following the tradition set by his father and his grandfather, apply for a place in the police force and hope someday to rise to a position as elevated as chief sergeant— but that was really far too much to hope for. As one of legions of men, all of them virtually indistinguishable to most white employers, he would have to keep his expectations on a much lower plane.

CHAPTER TWO

▼

We laughed during those occasions, same as the child of Africa laughs when it is lost and asks the way . . . we would laugh same as you say how absolutely funny when you mean how absolutely atrocious and abominable.

TODD MATSHIKIZA
Chocolates for My Wife[1]

[T]he smile policy is one of careless ease, its convenience is contained in the fact that the African cannot at this moment afford to lose his temper, so he must joke about the things which give him the most pain.

BLOKE MODISANE,
Blame Me on History[2]

Ngema stalled in Hlabisa for as long as possible, furiously playing music with Johannes and other family members, day and night, but he couldn't postpone the harsh reality of labor—prisonlike dormitories, regimented leisure—forever. Ma Hadebe was consumed now with nursing her husband, stretching his pension to keep their youngest children in school, and working the farm; her burden had doubled, and she was as pragmatic and unremitting as ever. She admonished Ngema to look for work at some factories she'd heard about from friends and from Johannes, who had visited a few himself in his own search for employment. And Ngema at last felt compelled to make a serious effort to find a job, with the keen understanding that the odds weren't in his favor. From Johannes he knew about the indignities he could expect to experience on the overcrowded work trail. Only his ancestors could help him find a position, he felt, and only if they were inclined to use on his behalf their influence with destiny.

First he went to the nearest pass office to apply for the reference book and work-seeker's permit he was now required, as an eighteen-year-old, to carry with him everywhere. He was instructed to undress completely with other applicants in a room where he was x-rayed and publicly inspected for venereal disease by a white examiner. (Later, in *Asinamali!*, Ngema created a character who similarly leaves Zululand to get a work permit and expresses the humiliation Ngema must have felt at this invasion: "No one has ever seen my man, except my older wife," he says in shame.) The permit allowed Ngema three months to look for a job, and only in a circumscribed area in the locality of the office. If he was still out of work when it expired and he was stopped by a policeman demanding to see his pass, he would most certainly be arrested.

One Friday morning, Ngema took his father's pickup truck and a brother to do the driving, and he went to look for a job in Empangeni, on the industrial Natal coast. The road from Hlabisa cut across the Umfolozi/Hluhluwe game reserve, where rare white rhinoceroses plodded through the brush, zebras abounded, lions dozed with one eye open, and, barely distinguishable from the tall vegetation swaying sleepily on distant hills, giraffes bowed down to feed on the loftiest trees.

Ngema napped nicely through this scenery, all the way to the vicinity of Mtubatuba, where the truck came to a sudden stop. As he tugged himself awake, he saw just ahead on the road a big black Mercedes-Benz and heard a stern male voice sputtering in Afrikaans: "What do you think you're doing? You nearly killed me."

Ngema had experienced little direct contact with white people in his eighteen years and, because Natal's European population was mostly British in origin, none at all with Afrikaners. He and his brother sat paralyzed and speechless, while the man reached his thick red arm in through the window on the driver's side, disengaged the engine, removed the key, dropped it in his pocket, strode to his Mercedes, and drove off without another word.

Forty-five minutes later, the police arrived, put the Ngemas in the back of their van, and delivered them to the Mtubatuba station, while another officer followed in Zwelikhethabantu's pickup truck. Ngema was the first to enter the station. The big Afrikaner was leaning against the front desk, chatting with a cop. He turned to Ngema with the underwater motion of the giraffes in the game reserve, set his gaze heavily upon him, raised a finger, and pointed. "Ja," he said, and then turned and vanished again.

Satisfied by the Afrikaner's pronouncement, the police charged Ngema with reckless driving and released his brother. Both Ngemas tried to explain the mistake, but no one would listen. "You'll have a chance to defend yourself in court," an irritable policeman snapped. The brother regretfully returned in the truck to Hlabisa, leaving Ngema in jail to wait for the magistrate.

Over the weekend, Ngema learned from an inmate that his Afrikaner was the retired commandant of the station. On Monday morning, awaiting his turn in court, he sat on a bench and watched with resignation as his accuser shared in a familial tête-à-tête with the magistrate. After the Afrikaner, in the witness box, had discharged a long, breathless tirade in inscrutable Afrikaans, he briskly left the building. In the words of Kenyan novelist Ngugi Wa Thiong'o, "Now tell me who is that man who can win even if the angels of God were his lawyers."

Ngema was called next. He tried to explain that he hadn't been the driver of the truck but failed to impress his innocence upon the court. He was summarily sentenced to one hundred days or a 100-rand fine, which he certainly didn't have and couldn't dream of raising, and then taken post-haste to a large prison in Empangeni, which, like most South African jails, resounded with "black laughter"—a coined phrase, familiar to all black South Africans who had ever said, as once did the journalist Todd Matshikiza, "how absolutely funny" when they meant "how absolutely atrocious and abominable."

In the morning, when Ngema awoke to the reality of his circumstance and began to search within himself for the means to abide it, a guard called his name, led him outside, and told him he'd been "bought" as a laborer by a white farmer. Ngema climbed in the back of a flatbed truck loaded with twenty other detainees, some of them women, charged with petty crimes like *staan en kyk* (stand and look; loitering), drinking in public, and failure to produce a pass.

Bouncing through the open air, Ngema rode deep into some of the most fertile—and therefore white-owned—farmland in all Africa, a landscape of steep, lush hills tumbling upon each other with the weight of their bounteous banana groves, sugarcane, and pumpkins. It was in this region of Zululand that in 1838 the Zulu king Dingane invited Piet Retief into his kraal for a friendly drink of *mtshwala* (Zulu beer). Retief was chief commandant of a group of independent-spirited Afrikaners who'd trekked from the British-administered Cape Colony to settle in Natal and sought a concession of land from the Zulus. Dingane privately distrusted him, and he was right to; concession or no concession, Retief's people would take the land. Once Retief and his unarmed men entered the kraal, they were clubbed to death by Dingane's warriors, who then attacked their camps on the Tugela River, killing nearly three hundred more Boers and two hundred of their Khoikhoi slaves.

Ngema knew this story well; vibrations from the past might have comforted him as he chugged helplessly through this landscape, except that directly northwest of Dingane's kraal was the spot where, ten months after Retief was wiped out, another faction of Afrikaner *voortrekkers* retaliated with guns and cannons. Some three thousand Zulus were killed in what the whites triumphantly named the Battle of Blood River. Every year on December 16, Afrikaners commemorate that victory and reiterate the pledge they first made more than one hundred and fifty years ago: "Here we stand before the holy God of heaven and earth to make Him a vow: that if He will protect us and deliver our enemies into our hands, we will observe the day and date each year as a day of thanks."[3]

The farmer showed Ngema and the others the sugarcane fields—once Dingane's domain—he had hired them to tend at a wage of 1 rand per day, payable at the completion of their terms. He took them to a compound on the plantation that was to be their home for the duration of their sentences. Because it was late, he told them, they would have to wait until morning to exchange their clothes and belongings for burlap tunics and bush knives. They were fed stony samp and cold coffee and locked inside with an armed guard.

For those whose only alternative was homelessness, this was a preferable arrangement. But Ngema believed he could do better and quickly decided not to accept the contract. A breakout would be nearly impossible after he surrendered his clothes and shoes, so he had no time to waste. That night his fellow inmates brewed some beer, sang, and talked about the strange heartlessness and humorlessness of white people, a topic of unending fascination, mystery, and black comedy. In order to hide his intentions from the guard, Ngema pretended to get drunk. Then, shortly after midnight, when the whole place was deep in intoxicated sleep, he and another man escaped from the plantation, walking for half a day along precipitous, unlit, unfamiliar roads. When he arrived again in Empangeni, Ngema collapsed in exhaustion on a curb. Then, to avoid a charge of loitering, he quickly pulled himself up again and tried to hitch a ride back home.

In an instant, a woman who recognized him from his bricklaying days at Mtubatuba stopped and gave him a lift. It seemed to him that *amadlozi,* the ancestors, were looking out for him. As so often in the years that followed, his angel came in the form of a woman.

▼

Between Empangeni and the Indian Ocean, a burgeoning of new industry had taken root in a place called Richard's Bay, where a new harbor was under construction, from which coal and other minerals would soon be exported. Ngema had a relative there, working at a massive aluminum refinery, and that's where he decided next to look for a job.

Fifteen years later, at the height of South Africa's summer, when the temperature outside had easily reached one hundred degrees, an Afrikaner foreman told me it would be far too hot inside to have a tour of the plant. "Let me put it this way," he explained pedantically. "People who come here looking for work now, in there, are *very* desperate people. The *heat,*" he said, with a gesture to his brow intended to send the message home. "You don't want to go in there."

The subtropical heat was probably just as dizzying when Ngema first visited the plant in 1975, hoping to profit by his relative's connections. But the facility looked somewhat different then than it does today. Where there is now a parking lot there was once an immense workers' compound—blocks and blocks of residential barracks and recreational areas for the company's thousands of black employees. To enter the compound, one had to present an ID card to a guard at the gate. When a visitor arrived, the name of the employee he wished to see was broadcast on a public-address system that infiltrated every alcove.

Ngema's man appeared at the gate half an hour after the guard sent his name ringing through the corridors, past all the cell-like dorm rooms. He was elated to see Ngema and took him inside to the heart of the complex and the tiny chamber he shared with six other men. They sat and talked, and the smoke from their communal cigarette fogged the room and their heads. Ngema began to hear beautiful guitar music wafting down the hallway and, enchanted, asked where it was coming from.

"Oh, this is a wonderful place," his brother said, with the kind of hand-over-heart reverence one saves for one's alma mater, especially if it's an Ivy League school. "The bosses really care about us here. It's not like other factories."

He gave Ngema a tour of the compound and showed him the soccer ground, the karate ground, the boxing gym, the lounge where liquor and *mtshwala* could always be obtained, the chapel. "And here is our music room," he said with a flourish. "Instruments for everybody!" The windows were painted black, and the door was locked. He knocked and explained to the man who answered that Ngema was a musician, interested in joining the employee band. Inside, Ngema was immediately handed a guitar and asked to audition, and he made a strong impression on the leader of the compound's band.

For three months, Ngema stayed contentedly in this artificial environment while he awaited assignment as a hard laborer. He took a test to qualify for a clerical position as well, in case one was vacated. In the meantime, while the other men were at work, he spent the days in his brother's room, smoking *dagga* (marijuana) and practicing his guitar with a teen-aged musical virtuoso named Skhumbuzo, who was living with a relative too. Ngema's friends gave him coupons he could exchange for food in the company canteen. On the weekends, he and Skhumbuzo would rehearse with the band in the music room. The *mbaqanga* music they played would go out over the public-address system. Sometimes women vocalists would be imported from the white suburbs where they worked as domestics. The alluring sound of sweet female voices would draw the other men in the barracks to the music room. They would press their faces up against the blackened windows to get as close as possible to what Ngema was in a position to touch freely—something the beneficent management, in all their largesse, hadn't provided.

So went the strangely sweet, slow days of factory life until Ngema finally got a job as a storeman, a position that entailed the lowest level of unskilled grunt work, mostly carting heavy equipment from one department to another. His white shift boss treated the black workers beneath him like naughty children and was often inclined to issue severe punishments for minor infractions; his anger would sometimes induce him to urinate in a man's mouth—a penance he called "a shot of vodka." Ngema held the position for another three months, until one Friday when a friendly white manager called him to his office to deliver some very good news: a clerical post had opened up for which he was qualified. He was instructed to report to his new department on Monday at 8:00 A.M., not in his overalls but in a shirt and tie.

Ngema was thrilled. The new job meant more money and a more humane way of life. He wanted to make a good first impression. On Monday morning, he arrived a half hour early, at 7:30, the time he was accustomed to reporting to work for his former job, and waited outside his new station, well scrubbed and neatly dressed. Then, in an unfortunate coincidence, his former shift boss arrived with his crew to fetch some oil drums from the very spot where Ngema was waiting.

"What are you doing here?" the boss snapped, as Ngema tells the story.

"I'm a clerk now," Ngema said with careful delicacy.

"No you're not, you crazy kaffir. You're no clerk," he said.

"Yes, my boss, I am."

"Didn't they tell you not to argue with me?" the boss said. Ngema was afraid he'd be fired or punished if he persisted, so in his pristine white shirt and borrowed tie, he hoisted an oil drum and fell in with the other men.

At 8:15, the exalted overseer, a man named Van der Walt, who wore a gleaming white helmet with his name specially printed across the front, arrived at work. The angry boss went to him directly to report Ngema's haughty transgression.

After a few minutes, Van der Walt called Ngema to join them. "You're not a clerk," he said, dully, in Afrikaans.

"What?"

"You're not a clerk," he repeated with grudging effort.

The next day, the pleasant man who had delivered the news of Ngema's promotion summoned him back to his office. He apologized for the misunderstanding and then demoted him to the department that was most dreaded by all the men in the factory—the "pot room."

Ngema remembers the pot room as a wing of the plant one and a half miles long, with 2,220 enormous kettles in a row, stretching farther than the eye could see, and long trenches through which rivers of chemicals flowed. Inside the kettles, liquefied aluminum boiled like red porridge—"one drop on your flesh, and the flesh was gone," Ngema says—and emanated a stinging smoke that clouded the air. All up and down the column of kettles, men worked for just five minutes at a time; then they ran for the nearest window, the size of a porthole, for another five minutes. In this manner—five minutes of work, five minutes of air—they passed eight and a half hours every day.

Ngema heard many stories of men who died of lung disease after two or three years in the pot room. Because he had a vague but somehow motivating sense of a future for himself, one day in this hell was all he would endure. The next morning, he said *sala kahle* (goodbye) to each of his friends, and turning his back on the amenities and the Sunday sopranos, the bottomless vessels of *mtshwala,* and young Skhumbuzo, he moved on.

▼

Some young men in South Africa leave their families in the rural areas to look for work and never return out of shame that they've failed as providers. Ngema may have been homesick, but he was absolutely on

his own now and couldn't go back to Hlabisa until he had the means
to improve his family's life in some measure. He didn't even try to
communicate with his parents. Most young men in his position probably would have stayed in the pot room at Richard's Bay with the hope
of being moved to a more tolerable department sooner or later—at
least it was preferable to the mines, where the work was so miserable,
so hazardous, and so poorly compensated that it was always available.
Ngema was concerned for his health, but he was also prodded by the
kick to his ego. Men and women in South Africa regularly endured terrible degradation in order to keep even low-paying jobs (the average
annual wage for a black worker in manufacturing then was 805 rand[4]).
But something in Ngema was telling him to use his strength to resist
what most men in his position would have strained to tolerate. He
seems to have lacked the common South African trait of fatalism.

With 10 rand in his pocket, he moved on that winter to Newcastle,
a city at the foot of the Drakensberg Mountains, one of the coldest
spots in the country, where sometimes it even snows. He knew one
person there, slightly, and hoped to find him.

Arriving in Newcastle at ten o'clock at night, Ngema found his way
from the bus station to the workers' hostel at Iscor, the gigantic, state-
owned iron-and-steel corporation. There he planned to use his acquaintance's name to get his foot in the door, as he had done in
Richard's Bay. The instant he arrived at Iscor, however, he realized it
would be nearly impossible to find this man, whose name was a common one. It was like arriving in New York City and hoping to find a
Kaplan—without a phone book . . . or a phone.

Iscor was a stupendous city in itself. And spread out in front of the
gates to the employee hostel was a vast shanty town of hovels fashioned from scraps of corrugated iron, sheets of plastic, and cardboard,
no bigger than doghouses. Sleeping inside each hut were two or three
or four employment-seekers.

It was a time of sharp economic recession in South Africa, shortly
after June 16, 1976, the day on which the famous Soweto uprisings
commenced. The student revolt began as a protest against the use of
Afrikaans as the medium of instruction in black schools and against
the system of Bantu Education. The unrest sparked in the Johannes-

burg area and spread in all directions across the country. As schools were boycotted everywhere, masses of young workers flooded the job market—and the outskirts of Iscor.

Huddled against the freezing cold, the hovel-dwellers slept through the night, while traffic constantly ebbed and flowed from the gates of the hostel. Men who had no time in life for anything but work and sleep returned in buses from round-the-clock overlapping shifts and boarded buses to go to work.

Shivering on the perimeter of the squatter camp, Ngema took in the dumbfounding scene. All the clothes he owned were on his back— cotton shirt, gray cotton slacks, dust coat. His only pair of shoes— sandals—were not keeping his feet warm.

Suddenly a male voice called from inside one of the hovels, startling him. "Hey!" the man said. Ngema inched a little closer. "Hey, you. Get in. Let's sleep," the voice called, in Zulu. Ngema inched closer still. "Get in!" the voice said with finality. "It's cold here." Ngema's toes were numb, so he ignored his misgivings and crawled in beside the occupant. "I've been waiting for someone to come by all night," the man said. "Don't move, or the house will fall." Then, wedged together to share their body heat, they both fell asleep.

When Ngema awoke in the morning, he found that his host had already left for the day. Ngema went to the employment office, found a mob scene, and returned to the camp, where all the little huts looked the same to him. He couldn't find his previous night's lodging and never to his knowledge saw that man again. He assembled his own hovel and stayed there for two weeks, living on water and bread, which was all he could afford. He made several trips to the employment office but found the effort futile, so he began to spend his days standing by the gates to the hostel, hoping to spot his acquaintance on his way to or from work. It was the lowest point of his life and an episode he can't quite believe when he talks about it now. And then one day he saw a familiar face, someone he knew, vaguely, from Hlabisa and hadn't expected to see.

"You can't come in the compound," this man said. "Everyone wears a band around his wrist with his ID number on it, and you can't get in without one."

"Well, I can't fight that," Ngema said.

"But I have a brother, Isaac, who lives in Madadeni. I'll take you to him."

Madadeni was the black township just outside Newcastle. Isaac, who lived there in a four-room house with three other men, took Ngema in without question and for six months fed him, advised him, took him to the shebeens on the weekend, gave him money from time to time, and asked for nothing in return, not even an IOU. Ngema returned to Iscor every day to join the masses of work-seekers, and when he heard that the management was administering written tests for a few clerical positions, he was one of some five hundred men who turned up. When the results were posted, each man having been assigned a number corresponding to his rank in the testing, Ngema received number 2, for he had the second-highest score. He had every reason to believe that, at last, he'd found a decent job.

The manager instructed all five hundred men who took the test to stand in formation—like the cavalry on parade—in the order of their ranking, so that he could go down the lines and call each man forward until he had the five qualified clerks he needed. Ngema was the second man in the first row. Immediately after the manager examined and accepted the man in first place, a brawl broke out farther down the line, at number 20 or 21, as two men argued over their positions. The manager shouted for order and sent his clerk to settle the dispute. And it was a matter of miserable luck that when calm was at last restored, the flustered manager lost his place and called next the man with the third-highest score, passing over Ngema completely. It would have done no good to point out the oversight. Ngema knew such a display of self-assertion on his part, no matter how humbly tendered, would likely infuriate the man.

That was the closest he came to getting a job in the six months he stayed in Newcastle. He became so discouraged that he began to consider joining the police—it was a road that had never enticed him but now seemed to be the only one open. But attitudes had changed since the days when his father joined the force, and Isaac counseled him against enlistment. Biko's view, that black police were actively involved in propping up the apartheid system, was now widely held. Soweto, the locus of the current political unrest, was hundreds of miles away, but even in Natal, unarmed protesting schoolchildren were being arrested by police—many of them black—detained, tortured, and even executed as terrorists against the state. It was out of the question for Ngema to choose the path of his father and grandfather, and the notion soon passed.

When Ngema heard that more factories were being built in Richard's Bay, he decided to try his luck there again. Isaac took him to the bus at dawn, bought him a ticket, and wished him good luck. After the disappointments in Newcastle, Ngema was not optimistic. He had no idea where his life was leading, but perhaps *amadlozi* did. Later in life, Ngema would see the serendipity in this sequence of setbacks: if he hadn't been so miserably jinxed and unfairly overlooked for the job at Iscor, he never would have gone back to Richard's Bay, where he found himself at the gates of a newly established fertilizer factory called Triomf. He took another test and was instantly hired as a clerk. And it was there that a whole new world was about to open up for him.

▼

Ngema might have stayed at Triomf a lot longer than three months if he hadn't been so happy there in his job as a file clerk. A black man in South Africa had to be careful never to talk back to his employer, as we have seen, but he also had to be mindful not to wear his pleasure on his sleeve. For there were some white people who suffered a black man's happiness like a thorn in the foot and wouldn't rest until they plucked it out.

Ngema's work was delightfully mindless. When he completed it all—usually by 11:00 A.M.—he was free to practice his guitar until 4:30, when the workday ended. Furthermore, his new status made him highly attractive to women, who tended to prefer an employed man over an unemployed man, and a clerk over a manual laborer. In a country where extreme poverty and unemployment were pervasive, and women often pursued boyfriends just so they could be treated to a decent meal from time to time, Ngema was suddenly a hot commodity. And he enjoyed the privileges of his new stature to the fullest possible extent.

That Triomf was a new factory and somewhat unsettled may explain why Ngema was permitted to structure his own days. But even today— it's been sold and renamed—it appears, at least in the administrative offices, to be a relatively pleasant place to work. With only six hundred employees, it seems nearly homey compared to monstrous Iscor or the aluminum plant. When I inquired about a tour, a white manager in the front office summoned an obliging, assiduous middle-aged black man from the training and indoctrination department, who seemed stunned that anyone would be interested but was clearly pleased to demonstrate his expertise. With a schoolmaster's pointer and elaborate wall charts, he passionately described the process by which sulfate rock is transformed into sulfuric acid, which reacts with phosphate rock and then becomes phosphoric acid, which is granulated, packaged as fertilizer, and shipped to a few distant countries, including Japan. Sometimes, instead of phosphate rock, which comes from the Transvaal province of South Africa, Togo rock, from Togo, is used. The sulfate rock comes from Canada on a tanker, of which there is a proud model in the waiting room.

Reflecting nostalgically on the past, the lecturer said that, while there is only one other man in his department now, in 1977, before international sanctions against South Africa impacted upon the industry and business was still good, there were six. Ngema worked down the corridor in a small office. The lecturer remembered him but had a stronger impression of Ngema's cohort, the supervisor of the company cafeteria, a man named Lucky.

Lucky was a charismatic and unforgettable figure, who moonlighted as a singer in a local band. He was from Nqutu, a Zulu village seventy-five miles west of Hlabisa. Self-educated, he had, in spite of his rural upbringing, an innate quality of urbane sophistication. When he stepped out of his coveralls after work, he dressed in expensive European fashions. When he expounded on anti-apartheid politics, about which he was passionate, his language and his delivery were spellbinding. He was a magnet for attention, and he pulled Ngema into his inner circle.

Lucky had a limitless store of ideas and a particular ardor for theater. He was always contemplating a number of burning plot lines. He hadn't seen many plays but was inspired theoretically by Biko, who said that "whatever we do adds to the richness of our cultural heritage as long as it has man as its center. The adoption of black theater and drama is one such important innovation we need to encourage and to develop."[5]

Before he met Lucky, Ngema hadn't even considered the existence of theater. He'd studied a little Shakespeare in high school but had never seen a play, professional or amateur, in performance. After listening to Lucky's lectures on the subject, he still didn't know what to make of theater. His guitar was all he cared or thought about. Because he could play it on the job, and because his mind was free from the constant ordeal of destitution, this period of his life was a happy one.

In an office directly across the hall, however, there was a white clerk who bitterly resented Ngema's lightheartedness and tried to make him miserable. Although the man was employed on a parallel level, he was better paid than Ngema and automatically in a position of superiority because he was white. Officious and small-minded, he took Ngema's guitar-playing and good nature as a personal affront. He frequently conducted surprise inspections of Ngema's work station, as if to find it in disorder would improve his mood. But because Ngema was fastidious in his work and never left a paper out of place, the man always retreated in a desperate funk.

Then one day, as Ngema was working out some chords on his guitar, the man stormed across the hallway with a broom and ordered him to sweep the entire building. Sweeping didn't fall within the scope of his job description, but Ngema was glad to oblige him because he was bored that day. He swept thoroughly, with great energy and precision, and all the while he sang. He sang up and down the corridors. He sang and he swept and he sang. And the white clerk was so deeply appalled by Ngema's performance that he reported him to the managers in the main office. What he told them remains a matter of some mystery, but the outcome was irrefutable: Ngema was immediately asked to resign.

When Lucky heard that Ngema had lost his job, he decided to quit, too, and took the opportunity to devote himself full-time to his theatrical interests. He completed a script, assembled a company of actors, engaged Ngema as lead musician, and planned to rehearse for a couple of months before staging performances in black communities in the Empangeni area.

The play, a musical called *Isigcino* (The End), was about adultery and not in the least political. Lucky was a revolutionary at heart, but he hadn't been exposed to the current activity in South African protest or political theater, centered around Johannesburg and the Eastern Cape. The leaders of the main political theater movement in Durban, the nearest major city, had been banished to prison on Robben Island in 1975.

Lucky's only direct theatrical references would have been the apolitical plays typically performed in church halls, cinemas, and hospitals in black townships—vehicles for farce, melodrama, and the popular music of the time. The foremost practitioner of this theater was Gibson Kente, who, in 1966, began to write, direct, choreograph, and compose the music for plays that took the popular form to an exalted level. Kente assembled and rigorously trained a repertory company in a style of performance uniquely suited to the packed, unamplified churches and two-thousand-seat cinemas that they visited for one-night stands throughout the country. For a few years in the seventies, his work encompassed some political themes, but before and after that period he wrote domestic comedies and township melodramas, which were transcended by his splendid music and by the superb performances of his actors.

Lucky had seen some of Kente's plays and described them to Ngema. But when one of Lucky's actors became ill and Ngema took over for him, *Isigcino* was still the only play Ngema had ever seen. Soon after, however, he had the opportunity to see what was widely considered at the time to be the finest piece of theater ever created in South Africa.

Touring the country was *Sizwe Banzi Is Dead* and *The Island,* a program of two one-act plays written through improvisation by the white South African playwright Athol Fugard and the two black actors who starred in them, John Kani and Winston Ntshona. The production had traveled to cities around the world, including London's West End and New York's Broadway, where, in 1975, Kani and Ntshona won Tony Awards for their performances. When they returned to South Africa, they embarked on an extensive tour of the country's black townships and tribal homelands, passing through Empangeni while Ngema was performing there in *Isigcino.*

Ngema attended the play and saw, to his surprise, just two actors on a bare stage. They spoke very good English, in mellifluous tones, with precise diction. They neither sang nor danced. They spoke directly to the soul about ordeals and feelings that related directly to Ngema's own experience. Not even the history books he'd read in school had moved him so deeply. Only music and the Zulu legends imparted by his grandparents, which had charged the black Zulu nights with electricity, had come close. "This world and its laws allows us nothing, except ourselves," one character says in the evening's first scene. "There is nothing we can leave behind when we die, except the memory of ourselves. I know what I'm talking about, friends—I had a father, and he died."

The experience of acting in *Isigcino* had sparked Ngema's imagination; now after seeing *Sizwe Banzi,* as if someone had pulled a switch, his vital interest was instantly captured. He was irreversibly stagestruck. He would never again try to find a conventional job, and it would be years before he saw his family again. He was still without a sense of home but, suddenly, not without a sense of purpose.

▼

According to the family legend, the only man Zwelikhethabantu ever arrested was an infamous mass murderer named Msomi, aka The Animal of an Ax. Time and again, Msomi slaughtered women, extirpated their private parts, which he wore like bangles around his arms, and vanished into the bush. With every murder his renown grew. The police were stymied. Then Zwelikhethabantu, who was still in Verulam at the time, was enlisted in a massive dragnet operation. According to no more official source than Ngema and others of his family, it was Zwelikhethabantu who finally apprehended Msomi, somewhere near the beachfront in Durban, saying only, "Let's go." Msomi quietly acquiesced. "Okay," The Animal said. When he appeared before a magistrate, the legend goes, he was wearing "bangles" from wrist to shoulder on both arms.

Feeling that the story had great dramatic potential, Ngema told it to Lucky, who fashioned a scenario out of it, a kind of psychological character study. The curtain opens on Msomi, a normal young man in love with a beautiful, uninterested girl named Mbali. Msomi pleads for her love, offers her expensive gifts, speaks to her sweetly, but fails to win her affection. His mother advises him to find a new girl, but he is stuck on Mbali. From a spiritual adviser he receives a bottle of blessed water, which he is instructed to bathe in and to drink from in order to attract her. He does so, but the effect is adverse: when Mbali sees him now, she runs in terror. Next he consults a witch doctor, who senses that Msomi is supernaturally endowed and prescribes a potent medicine, which transforms him into The Animal of an Ax. Mbali is his first murder victim. Among the cast of characters there are many more victims and a persistent, heroic policeman who is hot on The Animal's trail.

Lucky wrote a script, and Ngema composed a score. They called the musical *Too Harsh* and were enormously confident and proud of their work. They felt it was ingenious, with great commercial potential. But Empangeni seemed far too small a town for the success they envisioned, so they decided to take their script to Durban.

Before the journey, they visited a Zionist spiritualist. She blessed some drinking water for them to carry on the trip and gave them two long pieces of cotton cloth that she anointed with an herbal potion. She told them that if they wrapped the cloth around their heads like North African turbans, strangers would be hospitable and money would come easily.

Before boarding the train, they knelt and prayed. They were filled with excitement. They were about to spend their final cents on train tickets, however, and knew only two people on whom they could call in the Durban area. They were in need of some divine assistance. During the ride they drank a lot of liquor, and with nothing except themselves, they headed toward the big city in high, indomitable spirits.

CHAPTER THREE

▼

Though we do not wholly believe it yet, the interior life is a real life, and the
intangible dreams of people have a tangible effect on the world.

JAMES BALDWIN[1]

Sporting their bizarre turbans, Ngema and Lucky headed to Clermont,
one of the cruelest black townships in the Durban area—an intemper-
ate, exposed network of shacks and smoke and sewage ditches and
matchbook houses and laundry lines. Speeding cars swerved to avoid
children playing in the unpaved roads. One sensed that there were
robbers and con men and gangsters about, a suspicion reinforced by
the omnipresent troops of red-cheeked young Afrikaner cops, who pa-
trolled the streets in their roving Casspirs and official yellow vans.
There were no shelters for the homeless in the township, no park
benches, no sidewalks, no cathedral steps to camp on. It was no place
to be stranded. Clermont was above all distrustful, wary of strangers.

Clermont's physical landscape clambers and plummets, dramatically
heightening the feeling of peril. Directions here, as in all the hilly places
in South Africa, are almost never proposed in terms of left or right but,
rather, "go up at the next corner" or "go down at the stop sign." The
hills upon which, or at the feet of which, houses have been perched, or
dropped, are preposterously steep. A visitor's progress to the front door
is usually either an extremely slow and laborious uphill climb or a precipitous muddy downward skid on his heels (or backside).

Ngema and Lucky chose to begin in Clermont because Ngema knew someone there—a fellow named Alan, with whom he'd played in the band in high school. When they found Alan they told him about *Too Harsh,* inducted him as a member of their company, and moved into his mother's house. Then they immediately set out on a casting mission.

Because his passbook carried neither a house permit to show that he was an official resident of the Durban area nor a special permit allowing him to look for work as a nonresident in the immediate region, Ngema's mere presence there was illegal. In fact he had no work-seeker's permit valid in any region whatever; without that, unemployment in itself was a crime. But Ngema had no intention of getting a job, regardless of the law. It might have been possible to find low-paying, under-the-table work, but it would not have fit into his new plans.

Ngema had remapped his life: He and Lucky would become professional theater artists. Unfortunately, there were no legitimate theaters in the black townships where he planned to make his name, and few forerunners in the field. And as a factory worker from Zululand who'd seen only two plays in his life—*Isigcino* and *Sizwe Banzi / The Island*—Ngema knew little about the craft or the business of theater. And he had no material support to count on at all. Still, he had no doubt that he and Lucky would succeed. He felt that he'd landed on something absolutely right. Taking some exhausting menial job to support himself until his chosen career took off would have fractured his concentration and broken the spell, the magic, of rehearsing the play he was committed to.

Through a friend of a friend of a friend, they heard about a woman named Thandi Zulu, who had organized theater workshops for children in nearby Umlazi township, where she lived. Ngema knew that if he and Lucky were going to survive, they would have to follow every lead to find hospitable strangers sympathetic to their ambitions. With this in mind, they visited Zulu at home and told her they'd like to attend one of her performances. Her group would be performing very soon, she said, at a Roman Catholic church in the J section of Umlazi. They thanked her and said they looked forward to seeing her again soon.

That meeting was the beginning of an indispensable association for Ngema, one of many he would cultivate and depend on for subsistence and encouragement during this next period of his life. In Thandi Zulu, Ngema found someone who, even in this habitat of dire material suffering and want, instinctively recognized what James Baldwin meant when he wrote that "the interior life is a real life."

Zulu, the mother of six children, was separated from her husband and employed as a saleswoman in a shop in downtown Durban. She was active in a local Methodist church and a longtime member of its choir. Earlier in life, she and her husband set up house in the Johannesburg area, and she became an enormous fan of Gibson Kente, whose headquarters were in Soweto. She volunteered to sew costumes for Kente and became one of his close friends. When she left her husband and moved back to Umlazi, her hometown, she was engaged by Kente to make the bookings for his company's tours of Natal. She did so for many years.

Even before the widespread school boycotts of 1976 radically increased the truency rate, Zulu was anguished to see children who couldn't afford to pay school fees loitering around Umlazi, killing time, waiting for trouble to come to them. She made it a practice to invite them to sing gospel music with her church's choir. Then one day it occurred to her to employ the knowledge she'd gleaned from Kente. She wrote a play called *Thuliswa,* recruited children from the streets as actors, and mounted a production. The experiment was highly successful. In the years that followed, she wrote additional scripts and remounted *Thuliswa* with new children many times.

After Ngema saw Thandi Zulu's play, he visited her at home and presented a detailed critique. He was a stranger to her, with no credentials whatever, a penniless kid. But she invited him inside and listened to him with great interest, which was the proper, respectful thing to do.

To the Zulu people—especially in Natal, where the African population is almost uniformly Zulu and relatively conservative—"respect" is an essential concept with far-reaching applications. There is nothing Zulus value more than politeness in others. In turn, they will never rush you, they will always be extremely patient, and they will never turn you away from their homes. These hospitality conventions apply generally to all black South Africans but are especially characteristic of Zulus.

Deep in rural Zululand, where nobody is in much of a hurry, people can be a little plodding and grandiloquent in their speech. When they have guests, they like to sit and talk allegorically for long stretches, gesturing to God and to the ancestors at regular intervals. A foreign visitor will be treated to the most generous hospitality imaginable and may not want to leave; one who has an appointment elsewhere will have difficulty finding a polite means of extrication. "Westerners," wrote Steve Biko, "have in many occasions been surprised at the capacity we have for talking to each other—not for the sake of arriving at a particular conclusion but merely to enjoy the communication for its own sake."[2]

Listening carefully to someone's discourse is one of the most meaningful ways to demonstrate respect for that person. Zulus speak a great deal about the respect they owe each other and their ancestors, the respect to which they themselves are entitled, the respect they show to those they enter into contracts with, the respect their neighbors should show them. They have a custom called *hlonipha,* which is respect manifested as a kind of bashfulness. In the purest application, a married woman, who always covers her head in public, will *hlonipha* her father-in-law by also covering her shoulders with a scarf or shawl and keeping her eyes lowered in his presence; a man *hloniphas* his mother-in-law by never presuming to pronounce her name, addressing her only figuratively. On a number of occasions, I have seen a Zulu listening with the most delicate interest to a raving mad drunk who is pontificating incoherently; the listener would never dream of stopping the lecture, or calling the man a fool, or rolling his eyes, or doing anything but attend with a steady, considerate gaze and an occasional assenting "eh heh, eh heh."

It was with this respect that Thandi Zulu received Ngema, an unknown man young enough to be her son, as he ventured to advise her on her play. If Ngema hadn't also demonstrated the same respect to her—a gentility she recalls today with a girlish smile—she might have dismissed him. But she had a weakness for needy young people and found him especially charming. Ultimately, she not only applied his suggestions on how she might improve a certain choral arrangement and a few other details but came to regard him as a new son and would from that day feel a large degree of responsibility for his well-being. When he was hungry, he would always find a meal at Thandi Zulu's house.

▼

Soon Ngema and Lucky assembled a skeletal company and began rehearsals. A young woman named Mafiki, who lived in Clermont and showed promising talent, was willing to undertake all the female parts; Ngema would play guitar as well as the leading role of The Animal; Alan would also play guitar and take a role; and Lucky would act the part of the policeman.

Just as the work began, however, Lucky vanished. In Nqutu, some 125 miles up north, his mother had received news that her only son had been seen wandering indigently around Durban with his head wrapped in an absurd cloth. Scandalized, she sent her daughters in a neighbor's car to kidnap him in the middle of the night and deliver him to her. Lucky, who must have picked up his emphatic style and tenacity from his mother, was clearly helpless before her will, and seems to have gone without a struggle.

Ngema was momentarily staggered by Lucky's sudden disappearance. Lucky was the playwright, the one, between them, with the modicum of theatrical expertise. But Ngema had already slipped into the leadership role in their company. After Lucky's disappearance he did the only logical thing: he found someone to replace him.

Bheki Mqadi, a Clermont native, was eighteen years old but appeared to be twelve and had the voice of an angel. Ngema saw him performing in an amateur theatrical troupe, one like Thandi Zulu's workshop. Mqadi was ridiculously young to play the role of the police detective, but his voice was so sweet and his energy so magnetic that Ngema couldn't resist. Against the forceful objections of his mother, who was pursuing a university degree at the time and was a firm believer in the values of education, Mqadi dropped out of high school to join the *Too Harsh* group. Ngema was already an absolutist, intending to rehearse day and night, and he wouldn't engage anyone—no matter

that their services were voluntary—on an after-school or part-time basis. He promised Mqadi that his sacrifice would pay off in the end.
And Mqadi believed him.

Soon they enlisted two more actors, and the company of six rehearsed on the veranda at Alan's house until his mother complained of
the noise. Then they moved to a hillock that was bare but for a single
tree, beneath which they established their upstage and downstage, their
stage right and stage left. And the feeling Ngema had, they all soon
had—it was a fragile, crystalline feeling. They worked very hard and
they were destitute, but they had the luxury of youth, all the time in the
world, and all the hours in the day to make mistakes and correct them,
to make their play perfect. They paused only to look for a free meal at
noontime. Their day ended well after midnight, when they'd drink a little liquor and smoke some *dagga* before going to sleep. They were in no
hurry to perform in front of an audience, or to make money. They all
felt that there was a delicate enchantment about them, and they were in
no rush to break it.

Months passed before they booked their first public engagement.
They performed for a group of nurses at a hospital in Durban, in a
large lecture hall that seated about five hundred people, with no stage
lights or amplification. As the audience began to take their seats, there
was a flurry of nervousness onstage as the actors transposed the familiar rehearsal space on the hill to the blank performing space. A musician friend who had agreed to play accompaniment for the evening
was busy warming up; using the pedals of his drum set to keep the beat
on the high-hat and bass drum, he simultaneously played a compli-
cated guitar arrangement. And then the show began, and it proceeded
without a hitch. The nurses were gratifyingly appreciative; many were
moved to tears by some of the more poignant love scenes, especially
the ones between Mafiki and Ngema. Afterward, the company
counted their modest profits and celebrated their success in the
corrugated-iron, cardboard, and plastic-sheeting shack of Alan's
neighbor, a man named Fideles.

Although Ngema and Mafiki had playfully flirted with each other
since their first meeting, they had never allowed themselves an affair.
Even if Mafiki hadn't been engaged to be married to someone else, it

would have been important to both of them to keep the relationship professional for the sake of the show. But that night when they played sweethearts onstage they were acting out a real, long-suppressed attraction, which was intensified by the presence of a live audience and the heightened drama of the play. Ngema says they fell in love in front of those nurses. Later, at Fideles's house, feeling elated and liberated, they didn't hide their passion from the others. Alan in particular was furious with Ngema for yielding to a romance that would certainly upset the delicate balance of rehearsals. Furthermore, Mafiki's fiancé was known to have a murderous temper, which would unquestionably be exercised against Ngema if an affair should begin. "We've just seen our future! We've just seen how those nurses reacted, and you guys decide to be lovers!" Alan complained. "The show is going to fall apart."

Mafiki's mother was a "shebeen queen," who sold bootleg liquor out of the house Mafiki grew up in. Mafiki's brothers were *tsotsis* (petty gangsters). And Mafiki was engaged to a man with connections to the Clermont underworld. By all accounts, she was a spectacular actress with a natural gift for physical transformation, a lovely singing voice, and a heartbreaking way of showing emotion onstage. She was a tough young woman, but a captivating gentleness radiated through her shell, like the warm glow in an iron furnace. Although she was not conventionally beautiful, such were her charms that it was altogether conceivable that a man might commit murder for her.

Falling in love with Mafiki was an early indication of a recklessness that was not an aberration of Ngema's youth, a weakness he would outgrow, but a permanent condition. Undeniably, he is somewhat hedonistic by nature. But later in life, though he would sometimes succumb to jags of heavy drinking or smoking between productions, he would summon self-control in time to return to his work. No matter the consequences to himself or his lover, however, he has always found it nearly impossible to pass up any appealing woman, especially one who seemed to be attracted to him. His tender answer to the questions I've put to him about the numerous affairs in his life—many of which seem to have been highly irresponsible—is always the same: "But she loved me."

From the moment he and Mafiki became lovers, Ngema was a

marked man, never more than a step or two ahead of gangsters out to kill him—"That's the least they would have done," he says today. But somehow he always managed to slip past them. Once, Fideles went out of town and left the keys to his shack with Mafiki's brother. Mafiki snatched the keys so that she and Ngema could spend the night there alone. They slept on Fideles's narrow iron bed frame, without a mattress, without even a blanket, though it was winter. The shack was tucked behind some banana trees just past Alan's house. In the middle of the night, they heard some rustling in the trees and the sound of footsteps, but they thought nothing of it. In the morning, Alan told them that Mafiki's brothers had discovered she was missing and had gone to Alan's house to finally dispose of Ngema. On their way, they had passed directly by the little shack, rubbed right up against it, but by the grace of *amadlozi,* perhaps, they'd missed him again.

Alan, for one, became so distressed by the constant threat of violence that he dropped out of the play. By summertime, the fugitive couple was forced to recognize that the only way to save their lives was to leave Clermont. Although they had no prospects for lodgings and no money for cab fare, they decided to move to Umlazi, and walked some fifteen miles in the blistering heat to Thandi Zulu's house.

Ngema knew that Zulu wouldn't be able to invite them to stay—she and her children were living in her mother's house—but he thought she might know someone who could help them. To protect his pride, Ngema didn't tell her that they were homeless; he said only that they were looking for someone to replace Alan in the show. His hope was that the new actor would be in a position to extend his hospitality. Zulu thought of her next-door neighbor, a young woman who had a brother who might suit Ngema's needs. He lived in C section, a distant part of the township, with his mother, a social worker, who might be inclined to help them. After Zulu fed them, Ngema and Mafiki set forth again.

Among all the black townships, Umlazi ranks second in size to Soweto (which is actually an amalgamation of townships). As in most African communities, there are some decent, clean, middle-class homes amid Umlazi's desperate poverty, and a few pockets of affluence where the business elite have built rare two-story houses. Umlazi's most unexpected distinction is that, completely unlike barren Soweto and the other red-dirt, dusty Johannesburg-area townships, it has the capacity for resplendent natural beauty. Huge, shivering red trees cast orange shadows; beach umbrellas of purple blossoms stretch open over matchbook houses and shanties; giant aloes and palm trees assert themselves by the sides of unpaved roads. Cutting a deep gash through the township is the Umlazi River, on the banks of which children play among magical trees that are said to discharge tears of blood and cry like goats. At night, seen through squinted eyes from a summit, the township resembles the canyons of Los Angeles—white lights twinkling in the bushy hills.

By the end of the day, when Ngema and Mafiki arrived at the house in C section, they had negotiated on foot nearly all the ups and downs and recesses of Umlazi. The young man they sought wasn't home. But his mother, Margaret, invited them inside to wait and sent one of her other children to look for his brother. Mafiki and Ngema collapsed in chairs, feeling that they would never be able to move again.

Ngema made up a story for Margaret. He told her that they were waiting for a car to come and take them to Johannesburg, where they had been engaged to present their play. With that little lie he hoped to save face and at the same time persuade the woman that they were serious about their work and neither vagrants nor slackers. He feared that she'd doubt their integrity if she knew just how desperate they were and how urgently they hoped that they wouldn't have to walk out of her door before morning. Then Ngema began to play his guitar, and Mafiki sang along. Their hostess was enchanted.

Margaret was a widow, a thin, delicate-mannered woman in her late sixties. Her husband, James, had died some years earlier. She lived in her one-bedroom house with the fifteen children in her care, surviving on her husband's pension and the income those children who were old enough to work could contribute. She was a member of the local Anglican church and a volunteer at a Christian senior citizens' society.

One of her daughters, when she was young, had been known as the Zulu Shirley Temple, for she sang and danced in the manner of the child star. Margaret would take her to perform on the Durban beachfront, where white people vacationed in the luxury hotels that lined the Marine Parade. As the tourists strolled and admired the beads that Zulu women arrayed for sale on the promenade, some would drop a coin into a hat for a little girl singing "When I grow up in a year or two, I'll have a big surprise . . ." and "La Cucaracha" in the beastly sun. Occasionally Margaret persuaded the manager of one of the hotels to allow the girl to perform inside for what was called "silver collection"—a plate passed around the audience after the show for contributions.

Margaret had always had a tenderness for people who made music. When Ngema and Mafiki began to sing and, later, when the details of their homelessness came out, she wished, terribly, that she could help them. Ngema was perfectly polite, and so sincere and determined that it broke her heart to tell him that with all the children living with her, she couldn't possibly accommodate him in her home comfortably. But Ngema said she shouldn't worry about that; he and Mafiki would be perfectly comfortable there.

Soon after Ngema and Mafiki moved in with Margaret, they were joined by the rest of the company. The women slept in the bedroom with Margaret and the children; the men slept on the floor of the dining room. In the morning they ate cornmeal porridge with the family. At midday they appeared at the dwellings of friends, some of them a three-mile walk away, who would usually offer to share whatever they had on the fire. They could always count on Thandi Zulu for a meal if she happened to be home at lunchtime, but they often went for several days without eating anything but breakfast and a little dry bread later in the day.

Day and night the company rehearsed in Margaret's yard, luring curious neighbors out of their homes to watch. It became a matter of pride to Margaret that such people were staying with her. Some of her children resented sharing their cramped quarters and unfulfilling porridge, but they abided the inconvenience with good natures and few complaints.

After Ngema saw, at last, a Gibson Kente production at the nearby Umlazi Cinema, he began to rehearse the group even harder. *How Long?*, the play widely perceived to be Kente's masterwork, was then in its fourth year on tour. The two-thousand-seat cinema was packed, with no room left even to stand. There was drinking, smoking, and brawling in the house; babies bawled; Coke bottles flew; the audience roared, wailed, and laughed at the action onstage. The famous Kente actors were masterful at riding the cacophony like a wave. "When they make the noise, you hold them, then you come up while they go down," one of the actors, Mary Twala, tells me. Arguments broke out, knives flashed, vengeance was exacted, all before intermission. When the band launched into a musical number, the clamor swelled, people stood on their seats, the music surmounted the clamor, and then, above even the band, the unamplified voices of the singers blared. Kente had invented a special vocal technique and devised a performance style effectively combining elements of gospel, opera, Broadway comedy, and Kabuki to overwhelm in sheer life spirit the farce and drama generated by the audience.

Ngema's immediate response to the performance was to quit his own project. He felt that he would never match Kente's artistry. But his self-doubt was short-lived; he soon returned to rehearsals, hesitantly at first and then gradually becoming obsessed with equaling, in miniature, Kente's grand achievement. With the capacity for learning that is probably his greatest gift, Ngema took from that one experience in the Umlazi Cinema innumerable practical clues. He began running rehearsals straight through the night. If Mqadi fell asleep, Ngema would throw him into a cold shower. When they thought they'd matched Kente, they'd say, "He can't touch us now!" to cheer each other on.

Margaret observed how hard they were working and wished that they could turn their effort into a little profit. She went to the manager of a hotel on the Durban beachfront, where she'd once taken her daughter to perform, and asked if *Too Harsh* might play for his guests. The manager put her off, telling her to come back another time. She returned persistently until he finally said yes: he would allow Ngema and his company to perform, once, for silver collection.

Margaret found a shop that would rent musical instruments for the day, on credit against their earnings; she found a driver who would transport them in his van on the day of the performance, also on credit. Ngema engaged musicians, promising them a share of the pot as compensation for the earnings they'd lose by taking the day off from their regular jobs. On the appointed day, the expanded company packed themselves into the borrowed van, drove into town, and pulled up in front of the hotel. In their finest, cleanest clothes, Ngema and Margaret strode into the elegant lobby and brightly asked to see the manager. But when the man finally appeared, he said gruffly and without explanation, "I'm sorry, but blacks are no longer allowed to perform in this hotel," and sent them away.

Afterward, Ngema absorbed harsh words from the driver, from the man who'd leased the instruments, and from the musicians. Margaret felt responsible for the mishap and wanted to make it up to him. A few days later, she came home with exciting news: her neighbor Sam, a local businessman, wanted to hire *Too Harsh* to perform at a birthday party for his four-year-old daughter. It's difficult to imagine a play about a mass murderer, a mutilator of women, as suitable fare for such an event, but it apparently had all the elements of suspense, comedy, and sentiment that children require for their entertainment. The young audience was delighted. And the adults in attendance were equally enthusiastic, no one more than Sam, who, with a finely tuned business sense and an eye for a good investment, saw the commercial potential in *Too Harsh* and decided to promote it.

CHAPTER FOUR

▼

[In the Indian villages in Mexico, the] people who earn the most money know instinctively that to buy material things with that money would not be very interesting but to buy prestige is marvelous. . . . Therefore they buy fiestas. . . . Their earnings go whoosh into the sky, but their fiesta is that much grander than the next man's and so they get more prestige. . . . All is cyclic: a matter of circles and periodic explosions. If some people earn more money there is a bigger fiesta, if they earn less, there is a lesser fiesta. But the rhythm is constant: increasing, accelerating excitements culminated by the outburst. This is what I mean by necessary.

PETER BROOK[1]

Sam made his entire living from the few *kombis* (minivans) that he owned and operated as group taxis between Durban and the C section of Umlazi. If it hadn't been for his neighbor Khassi, who operated taxis along the same route, he would have had an exclusive claim to C-section riders. The two men had occasionally found themselves embroiled in professional rivalries, but before Ngema came between them, they usually managed to strike a friendly compromise. Today they must strain to be polite when, by accident, they meet.

Khassi worked by day for a dry-cleaning company and ran his taxis on the side. His wife, Bongi, was an obstetrical nurse. Their combined income was above average and, as they had no children, amply supported them and paid for the housekeeper who lived with them in their neat four-room house. Their furniture was handsome, their garden well tended. In addition to the *kombitaxis,* Khassi owned an old

Jaguar, a Toyota Cressida, and two Ford Valiants. Furthermore, Khassi and Bongi were not only moneyed—by township standards—but warm, generous people. Before going to Sam, Margaret had tried to enlist them as Ngema's patrons and promoters. But although they were interested by what she had to say about *Too Harsh,* the timing was unfortunate. Khassi's sister had just died, and their mourning observance precluded them from having guests or taking part in any activities outside their home for a period of three months. They told Margaret that if Ngema could wait, they might be able to help him later on. But Margaret could no longer support the troupe, and for Ngema's sake as well as her own, she wanted to find a sponsor immediately. Sam, known for his interest in sly investments, was her second choice.

Commercial expansion by Africans was subject to severe limitations imposed by municipal authorities to protect white businesses. Minor adjustments were made periodically to loosen and tighten and loosen again these restrictions, but generally entrepreneurs like Sam and Khassi could operate businesses only in the black townships. Even then they could provide only a narrow range of services and goods— almost all of which had to be obtained from white wholesalers— defined as necessities. Before starting a new enterprise, they were required to apply for a trading license, and they weren't allowed to operate more than one business. They couldn't build or own buildings, form partnerships, or pool resources. To purchase any item or service beyond the bare essentials, township residents were compelled to travel to the city, to white or Indian merchants. Because there were so few shops in the townships, it was common (and still is) for people to run under-the-table sidelines out of their homes, such as selling cold soda pop or men's overcoats.

Sam began his career as a bus driver for Putco, the state-run transit authority, and resided in a Putco hostel. Because the management provided a number of sports facilities to keep its impounded workers busy during their free hours, Sam learned to box, a skill he makes profitable use of today, in training and managing the careers of some ten young boxers. When he left Putco, he was seized by an ambition to go into business for himself and, from the few trades open to him, chose taxis. Later, after his encounter with Ngema, he ran a butcher shop in Pietermaritzburg. Today he controls a small shopping complex in Umlazi, where he personally operates the sparely stacked general store and rents out a butcher's and a tailor's shop. All that remains of the taxis he once owned are the trading licenses, which he leases to others from time to time.

Sam's capitalistic urges were often frustrated by government restrictions. He was always on the lookout for creative ways to circumvent the law and to exercise his business acumen. Becoming a theatrical promoter struck him as a perfect solution; because there were no white producers vying for township audiences, the government had no interest in legislating against black producers. Sam knew that Gibson Kente, an exemplar for the black entrepreneur, could sustain the run of a popular play for years and usually had more than one play touring the country at a time. When television was introduced in South Africa in 1976, Kente began to make TV films, as well, and employed hundreds of people. There was still room for a few semiprofessionals, who were managing to eke out a decent, if unstable, living from "showbiz"—a widely used term embracing all forms of South African entertainment, high and low—if not on Kente's level. Today Sam says he was only giving Ngema a hand, as a humanitarian, but it seems likely that he envisioned some grandeur for himself as a township impresario. Although his involvement with Ngema was his first and last foray into showbiz, he may indeed have had a gift for it; he certainly had a good eye for talent, for Ngema has, in the end, far surpassed even Kente's attainment and prestige.

When he met Ngema, Sam was looking after a house left behind by a friend who had gone to prison. He installed the *Too Harsh* company in a room there, pledging them one bag of groceries a week, and went about seeking engagements for the show in hospitals, schools, and church halls all over Natal. He had high hopes going into the venture and put a great deal of energy into promoting the play. He probably made a little profit—somebody must have, and it wasn't the actors, who received nothing beyond their lodgings and groceries, or the musicians, who were paid only occasionally. But Sam did have substantial overhead expenses—he bought a *kombi* just to transport the cast and equipment around, and a few secondhand instruments to supplement the band—and the show never turned the profit he'd hoped for.

Sam was disheartened by the financial disappointments, but it was when he began to feel that he wasn't earning the respect he believed he was entitled to that his relationship with Ngema became antagonistic. To those around him, it seemed that Sam was growing increasingly galled by the fact that Ngema was getting all the acclaim for the enterprise. In Sam's mind, whoever took the financial risks deserved the prestige and acknowledgment. But everywhere they went, it was Ngema who received the applause, and it was Ngema who had the authority over the actors. When Sam booked the troupe at a hospital to perform for nurses, among them a woman he wanted especially to impress, he decided to seize the moment and the stage. On the afternoon of the performance, he bribed the musicians with beer and food and, behind Ngema's back, planned a performance of his own that was to come at the tail end of the show, at which time he would make it clear to everyone present that he was the power behind *Too Harsh*. But when the nurses filled the hall and the lights went down, he must have experienced a surge of stage fever that he couldn't resist: Before the actors could make their entrances, Sam suddenly appeared before the audience like a celestial vision, in a snow-white three-piece suit. He turned to the band and counted, "One, two, three, four." The musicians began to play as Sam had instructed them earlier (Ngema recalls a *bossa nova;* Mafiki says it was "Remember Me"; and the guitar player says they played a blues tune). Ngema, standing dumbfounded in the wings, heard: "Here comes Bra Sam, ladies and gentlemen! I just want to tell you that I'm the boss here. I'm the one who organized everything!" Then Sam executed a jaunty tap-dance routine he'd learned when he was in grammar school.

Ngema was outraged. The next day, he paid a visit to Khassi and Bongi, whose mourning period had just ended. And shortly, bitterly, he left Sam.

▼

Khassi was thirty-four years old, bearlike and handsome, with a faint roguish glint in his eyes and a penchant for risk-taking. When approached by Ngema, he had been considering an offer from an uncle to start a business in Mozambique and had just returned from a visit to that country. This was just three years after independence, and almost ten years before President Samora Machel was killed when the plane he was flying in crashed in South Africa, under questionable circumstances. Khassi was overwhelmed by Mozambique's then paradisal—now devastated—beauty; the orange trees lining the streets, heavy with voluptuous, tender fruit; cashew nuts strewn everywhere like fallen leaves; and, in the Mozambique Channel, fish in such abundance that fishermen could catch them with their bare hands. Khassi decided that he would like to live in such a place. But as soon as he returned home to discuss the possibility with Bongi, he was visited by an earnest, skinny young man—Ngema. And before he knew it, the young man and his friends had moved into his home. Soon Khassi was doing his weekly grocery shopping for fifteen people.

Khassi and Bongi had built a decent life in the midst of widespread indignity and distress, but they were only a slippery step above the poverty line, and only for as long as they had no responsibilities beyond themselves. After they entered into Ngema's world, it didn't take long to lose the slight advantages they'd accrued. To subsidize *Too Harsh,* it very soon became necessary for Khassi to sell off all his personal cars and his taxis. And he would never again be able to consider leaving Umlazi.

When Ngema met Khassi and Bongi, he was deeply moved by their warmth and generosity. Bongi, he recalls, was one of the most intelligent women he'd ever met. Sam had regarded Ngema as a commodity, but Bongi and Khassi treated him as an honored guest. He admired their taste in beautiful things, especially their sofa and matching chairs, upholstered with red velvet cloth in dark oak frames, an upscale version of a style that is found in variations in black homes all over South Africa.

The period that followed was a time of cooperative effort and mutual sacrifice that is virtually unimaginable in America. There could be no benefactors anywhere more dedicated and unhesitating in their generosity than Khassi and Bongi. Because they were childless, they had a wealth of untapped affection. Khassi wasn't old enough to be Ngema's father, so he assumed the role of a protective elder brother. He arranged tours for the show, as Sam had done. On his day off, he drank a little brandy as he watched the company rehearse in the yard under an avocado tree. He took Ngema to a music shop, where they chose brand-new instruments to equip a band that Ngema was expanding to match the sound of Gibson Kente's. He retained an entire brass section. He bought costumes and hired transport, and bit by bit, the personal assets he and Bongi had acquired began to disappear. Every now and then, Khassi would entreat Ngema to get a paying job. But when Ngema would say that he simply could not do so, as the show required his constant concentration, Khassi would quickly accede. He bought a cot so that Ngema wouldn't have to sleep on the floor. And he let him take his one remaining car out for a drive. When Ngema dented it, Khassi scolded him as an older brother would.

Khassi had attended Kente's plays when they'd been presented in Umlazi, but only because the crowded cinema was an enjoyable place to drink and socialize with his friends. He had never considered theater as anything but a burlesque. *Too Harsh* had only the weight of melodrama, but because he saw that Ngema and his actors approached their work with Zen-like dedication, Khassi came to think of theater as a sacred vocation. When he saw his neighbors gathered around the yard, listening to Mafiki, Mqadi, Ngema, and the others sing, he was as proud as he'd ever been. He harbored the idea that Ngema might be successful someday, like Gibson Kente, and return his investment, but in the meantime he lost all his equity and never held out any reasonable hope of a profit, and the boon to his pride was temporary reward enough.

Their hard work was to culminate in two major performances, which Khassi scheduled a week apart. For the first performance he rented the two-thousand-seat cinema where Ngema had first seen Kente's *How Long?;* for the second show he rented a fully equipped theater facility in a white hotel on the Durban beachfront. Khassi bought ads in the major newspapers to promote the hotel performance. For the cinema engagement he had banners painted and hung all around Umlazi and the neighboring black townships, and he hired a *kombi* with a loudspeaker to advertise in the streets.

News of the performances reached far and wide—all the way to Hlabisa, where Ngema's family saw an announcement in a newspaper.

The last time he'd seen his parents, before leaving for the aluminum factory in Richard's Bay, Ngema had never even attended a play. His parents were amazed and mystified by the sight of his name in a newspaper. People also read about *Too Harsh* in Nqutu, where Lucky and his mother lived. But Lucky wasn't pleased or excited about the news of Ngema's apparent success; as the author of the script, he was disturbed to find that his name was mentioned nowhere in the publicity. And just as suddenly as he'd vanished from Ngema's life, he decided to reappear.

Coincidentally, Lucky's neighbor in Nqutu was married to Sam's sister. Lucky and Sam had met on numerous occasions over the years and were friendly acquaintances. As soon as he heard about the upcoming performances in Umlazi and Durban, Lucky went to Umlazi to pay his friend a visit and to seek his business advice. Sam, still embittered by Ngema's abrupt and undiplomatic desertion, agreed with Lucky that it had been unethical for Ngema to proceed with the play without permission. He urged Lucky to take decisive action. Sam confronted Khassi, and many harsh words were exchanged, though no resolution was reached. Khassi, troubled by the meeting, hoped that the controversy would blow over and decided not to risk upsetting Ngema by telling him about it. In the meantime, Sam put Lucky in touch with a lawyer.

Then, two days before the cinema engagement, Ngema answered a knock at Khassi's door. "Lucky! Where have you been?" Ngema exclaimed. Lucky didn't answer; impassively, he invited Ngema to accompany him to a car parked in front of the house. Sitting in the front seat was a stranger, a lawyer, who drove them to the Executive, the only hotel in the township, for a formal meeting. The lawyer then showed Ngema some official-looking papers documenting the fact that Lucky had legally registered *Too Harsh* under his own name. If Ngema went forward with the play, the lawyer told him, the police would stop the performance and arrest him.

Lucky had no interest in revenues or royalties; morally outraged that Ngema had claimed full authorship, he simply didn't want the play performed. If Ngema had ever met a lawyer before, he might have had the presence of mind to try to appease Lucky by offering him a share of the proceeds, but he was too intimidated to think clearly or negotiate. When the meeting ended, he returned to Khassi's house and told everyone that the show was canceled. Khassi would have to forfeit his marketing outlay as well as the rental fees for the cinema and the hotel.

When he went to bed that night, Ngema believed that he had no alternative but to forget his whole year's work. But in the morning, his outlook changed. While there was nothing he could do about the performance that had been scheduled for the next day in the cinema, for which a disappointed audience was bound to show up, he could write an entirely new play in time for the hotel engagement.

In a week, he scripted, composed, and rehearsed a new musical, called *The Last Generation*. Ngema had become much more politically conscious since coming to the Durban area, where the fashionable hairstyle was an Afro, bell-bottoms were in, and the youth talked proudly, as they did in America, about the beauty of the African race. The politically motivated plot he constructed for the new play concerned children who fled the country after the Soweto riots to go to guerrilla training camps in Tanzania; children who, Ngema optimistically projected, would be the last generation of oppressed people born in South Africa. Ngema and his cast worked frantically in Khassi's yard, and when their date to perform at the hotel arrived, they were ready. Lucky vanished again, without a word to Ngema.

▼

Ngema had begun to explore the theatrical scene in Durban, attending plays and recitals of politically oriented poetry, which influenced him in the writing of *The Last Generation*. At the Stable Theatre Workshop, he saw a play called *Working Class Hero,* which particularly excited him. It had been written and directed by an Indian, Kessie Govender, who also starred. Govender, an extraordinary poet and iconoclast, had built the Stable from the foundation up, with his own hands. In addition to mounting his own work there, he offered classes in acting, directing, and speech, and sometimes produced the work of other playwrights and oral poets.

Working Class Hero presents, naturalistically, a Durban construction site, where conflict arises between three Indian bricklayers and their

African subordinate. The African worker, paid far less than the Indians, is exploited and insulted by them. He fetches cold drinks and cigarettes at their command, and while the others take tea breaks and moan about their hangovers, he performs the skilled labor they're supposed to be doing. In a nation of unreasoning partisans, for whom euphemism and rhetoric had always come more easily than reform (viz., the government agency charged with enforcing the harshest racial laws, originally called the ministry of Native Affairs: the government renamed it Bantu Affairs, then Non-European Affairs, Plural Relations, and finally landed on the innocuous and misleading Cooperation and Development), Govender's use of unaffected urban speech and very realistic swearing seemed radical and staggered Ngema. The playwright made little attempt at lyricism and wasn't afraid to take a harsh look at the hypocrisies committed by people of his own race. Ngema had known many Indian people over the years, grown up on their food, shopped in their stores, but he'd never personally met one with Govender's outlook—one of open contempt for those Indians who complied with the government by accepting their place beneath whites and above Africans in apartheid's hierarchical design. When Ngema introduced himself to Govender and told him about *The Last Generation*, Govender invited him to mount the play at the Stable.

Govender remembers Ngema as a "hardworking and persistent person who utilized his energy very freely, never shirked from what he was doing, and never gave in. And, one way or another, he would get whatever he wanted." With the ineluctable charm and urgency that had dragged so many others into his service, Ngema would ask Govender for advice in building sets. Before he knew it, Govender was building the sets himself.

Years later, I had been warned that Govender could be a reticent and enigmatic person; maybe I'd even find him cold. But when I called him from my hotel in Durban to tell him that I'd arrived, he came directly over with roti freshly baked by his wife. He made me tea in my tiny room, and smoked and watched me while I ate and sipped. For the next few days he was always available to me. He took me to a meeting of the Theatre Alliance of Natal (TAN), a Cosatu/ANC–affiliated organization, where for several hours members of all races, representing every discipline of the theater, debated in the abstruse language characteristic of these organizations the final amendments to their constitution. Afterward, in the foyer, Ngema's newest play, *Township Fever,* which had just opened in Johannesburg amid well-publicized political controversy, was the subject of a heated debate.

At his cluttered flat in Sydenham, an Indian community, Govender declined to take a position in the argument. He gave me draft copies of fifteen-year-old plays with antique cigarette ashes crushed between the pages, photocopies of a column he wrote years before for a Durban newspaper, sheets and sheets of his poetry, and a copy of a story he'd been working on, a South African adaptation of "Jack and the Beanstalk." He talked of the similarities between the Indian and the African people, and the links between his vernacular, Tamil, and the Zulu language. The elephant, for both Africans and Indians, he said, symbolizes strength, compassion, tenderness, love, and fierceness. The betel nut is as popular in Zimbabwe as in India.

He said that in South Africa the artistic pulse tends to beat in men between the ages of eighteen and twenty-six and then dies out when they must apply themselves to family responsibilities. But in Ngema, as in himself, the energy still flows and will keep on flowing, and that they have in common. When I spoke, he listened with a small, beatific smile, leaning back in his chair, smoking a cigarette. Later, we talked about how amazing it is that man has the ability to stay here on earth and still know what's going on in outer space. "We are a minute particle of the sun," he said, "and the thread is slender."

▼

The most effective technique used to promote a play in the black townships was to post huge cloth banners in highly visible places. But marketing a play to a city audience required an entirely different tactic, completely foreign to Ngema. On the day that *The Last Generation* was to play at Govender's theater, Ngema had failed to reach his audience, and only one person sat in the auditorium. Ngema was compelled to cancel the performance. For a while afterward he tried to obtain funding to sustain the production from the Durban city council and met with some people from the cultural wing of Inkatha—an organization that didn't yet have the negative associations it later acquired—but every attempt was ultimately unsuccessful. Furthermore, Mafiki had decided to return to her fiancé, Mqadi's mother was demanding that her son return to school, and the company was unraveling again. Ngema began to sense that there was no future for him in Durban. He wanted to learn more about theater and decided that he would seek out South Africa's unrivaled master, Gibson Kente. From the brief encounter with Govender he'd learned something important about the naturalistic approach, but it was Kente's secrets, which were held in Johannesburg, that he now wanted.

He presented his plan to Khassi and Bongi. Although in knowing Ngema they had lost most of their material assets, they had been enriched by his presence in their lives. Their house, their lives, would seem emptier without him. But they had completely run out of money and could support no more of his high-priced theater projects. They agreed that the move was a good idea and gave him their blessing.

CHAPTER FIVE

▼

[T]he urge to rise and go out to do things, to conquer and become someone, the impatience of the blood, seized him. So he upped and went to Johannesburg, where else? Everybody went there.

CAN THEMBA[1]

After he had paid 13 rand for the train ride from Durban to the unknown frontier, Johannesburg, Ngema had only loose change in his pocket. When he arrived in the Jo'burg depot, there was a great deal more to the town than there had been when his grandfather was dispatched there in the early 1900s. Seventy-five years later, the city was an inhospitable place where even a native South African, whose lineage went back much further than Vukayibambe, was made to feel like a foreigner. There were no friendly porters, no maps readily available. What signs had been posted were written in English or Afrikaans—probably the only two South African languages Ngema didn't hear spoken in the crowded station. The overstuffed commuter trains that infiltrated the townships were not marked in any way to indicate their destinations or what stops they would make. Ngema had to ask a number of passengers for directions to Soweto, a vast teeming parallel universe of over a million people distributed among a complex of distinct communities, among them Orlando, Diepkloof, Pimville, Mofolo, Chiawelo, Zola, and White City. After he disembarked from the Soweto train, Ngema learned that Kente lived in Dube, and he made his way there on foot. He followed successive packs of children on their way to one school or another until finally, at eight-thirty in the morning, he found Kente's house—an unexceptional compact brick structure considered "posh" by township standards. Kente was still asleep. Ngema was invited by one of Kente's assistants to have a seat in the garage, where he waited while young men moved Kente's BMW out into the driveway, washed it with slow, painstaking thoroughness, rubbed it dry, and put it back.

Ngema had been awake all night, and suddenly, in the blurry daylight, he saw that there was a great deal to adjust to in his new environment. "First there were the ordinary problems . . . ," wrote Can Themba twenty years earlier of a similar moment of transition; "the tribal boy had to fit himself into the vast, fast-moving, frenetic life in the big city. So many habits, beliefs, customs had to be fractured overnight. So many reactions that were sincere and instinctive were laughed at in the city."[2] Ngema had lived in some of the toughest townships around Durban, but Johannesburg was a different, ruder bedlam. The exacting politeness with which people in Natal, even in the urban ghettos, still favored each other had largely fallen out of style in Soweto, especially among the youth, who were the arbiters of all substance and gesture in the wake of the student uprisings of 1976. And while Natal's African population was almost uniformly Zulu-speaking, in Soweto dozens of African languages were spoken, including hybrids blending Afrikaans and English in with the vernacular. Many Soweto natives born of Zulu heritage didn't even speak fluent Zulu. Still, in spite of the relative swagger and insouciance of the metropolis, and the awkwardness of having to establish a common language with every new acquaintance, an out-of-towner like Ngema could migrate to the front door of the number-one impresario in the country with only 7 rand to his name and expect to be treated with decency. Bra Gib, as Kente was familiarly called, was accustomed to uninvited visitors.

When Kente finally awoke and came outside, Ngema explained that he was an actor looking for work. They had actually met once before, he informed Kente, after one of Kente's performances in Durban. Kente apologized that he couldn't recall the meeting, and said that he was just about to send his newest show, *Taxi Man and the School Girl,* on tour and wouldn't be ready to cast a new play for several months. And then he returned to the house.

Outright rejection hadn't occurred to Ngema. He had nowhere else to go and sat down in the garage to think. A musician wandered in with a guitar and chatted with him. They showed each other a few chords. Then another musician came by, and they all jammed a little. Then a young man named Mali Hlatswayo, who was Kente's publicity director and made his bed on a foam-rubber mat beside the BMW, came and talked to Ngema. Soon Ngema was settling into the garage. It would be his home for the next three months.

Because the house was overflowing with actors and musicians, Ngema's residence in the garage went unnoticed by Kente for the first couple of weeks. But as soon as he loaded his tour bus and sent the show on the road, Kente became acutely aware that Ngema was there. He began sending daily messages to the garage, asking him to find somewhere else to stay. But Ngema had nowhere else to go and he chose to remain. Other hopeful actors came from Cape Town, Durban, and Pietersburg to ask for work and were turned away, and some of them moved into the garage for a while, but Ngema outlasted them all. Each morning when he saw Kente drive off in the BMW, he would come out of the shadows to be fed by a kindly housekeeper.

The work of Ngema's "roommate," Mali Hlatswayo, entailed painting banners advertising every one-night stand on the tour and hanging them above the most widely traveled roads. He had inherited the job from Darlington Michaels, who abandoned it to become an actor, one of Kente's best, but Hlatswayo seemed to have been born to write banners. As a child, he had enjoyed drawing, doodling, and making ornate designs from letters of the alphabet. As an adult, he loved spreading out an immense piece of soft cotton fabric—dyed black if possible—and applying bright colors with thick housepainting brushes. It was difficult to make the lettering neat and handsome with such a clumsy instrument on such a flimsy canvas, but Hlatswayo had perfected the technique. Today he is considered one of the great banner writers of all time.

Hlatswayo moved into Kente's garage when he was sixteen years old. He had no interest in becoming an actor, but he loved the music and camaraderie of Kente's work. He went to Kente and told him that he wanted to spend his life around the theater. Kente detected an innate organizational talent in the likable youth and agreed to talk to his parents who were delighted to let their son live with the famous and revered man. When Ngema showed up, Hlatswayo had been in residence for twelve years.

Ngema has told the garage story—how Kente tried to eject him and how Ngema held tight—to the South African press on more than one occasion. And Kente, who has had more than his share of public relation problems, hates it, because he thinks it makes him seem heartless. Largely because Ngema persists in telling the story, Kente has refused to speak to me about Ngema on the record. The end of the story, however, illustrates Kente's great generosity: In Ngema's fourth month in the garage, Kente finally asked him to sing; when he liked what he heard, he gave Ngema a bed in the house and told him that if he'd wait just a little longer, he'd have a part in the new play.

Although Kente would not allow our conversations about Ngema to be taped or directly quoted, he met with me numerous times and talked at length about his feelings concerning Ngema, about other young theater artists whom Kente had fostered, and about his own work. I visited with him both in his home and at the Orlando YMCA in Soweto, his base of operations, where I also attended a rehearsal and a performance of one of his plays. He was always warm and in every way accommodating.

It is well known that Kente grew up in the Eastern Cape, as a Xhosa speaker. In 1955, he went to Johannesburg, where he was employed as a social worker before pursuing his gifts as a composer and becoming a talent scout for the South African recording company Gallo. He wrote songs for the top performers of the day, including Miriam Makeba, Letta Mbuli, and the Manhattan brothers, who received only paltry fees and no royalties from the white-owned recording companies.

In 1959, a musical play that greatly inspired Kente, *King Kong,* opened in Johannesburg. The score was written in tonic sol-fa (the system of notation still used by most black South African musicians and composers, including Ngema) by a black composer, Todd Matshikiza. The entirely black cast included Kente's friends Makeba, the Manhattan brothers, and Mbuli. The rest of the writing and production team were white people, many of them amateurs and dilettantes—liberal industrialists and mining executives with creative streaks. The idea behind the play was to create a South African *West Side Story* meets *Porgy and Bess,* set in the fifties in the legendary multiracial township Sophiatown, long since razed, and featuring the sublime jazz music that marked the era. The story of the title character, King Kong, was taken from real life. He was, in Matshikiza's words, "a famous boxer, a notorious extrovert, spectacular bum. . . . He ate you up at the slightest excuse, for looking at him in anticipation of an acknowledging smile."[3] Kong was the champion on the "non-European" boxing circuit but was unknown outside of the black world. After his death, dozens of songs about him were recorded by black artists and released by the white-run companies on forty-fives. King Kong, in death, became a heroic figure. As mythologized in the plot of the musical, he is tormented by gangsters, kills one of them, murders his girlfriend out of jealousy, demands the death penalty for himself in court, and then drowns himself in prison after his plea is rejected.

Matshikiza was a multi-talented man, a journalist and composer who, to supplement his income in lean times, had also sold razor blades. The experience of working with the white production team, who reportedly rewrote his score behind his back, was to bring him to "the brink of a nervous collapse because I have been listening to my music and watch it go from black to white and now purple. . . . Every night I dreamed I was surrounded by pale skinned, blue-veined people who changed at random from humans to gargoyles. I dreamed I lay at the bottom of a bottomless pit. They stood above me, all around, with long, sharpened steel straws that they put to your head and the brain matter seeped up the straws like lemonade up a playful child's thirsty picnic straw."[4]

Matshikiza may not have seen his score realized exactly as he'd written it, and there's no telling how great a work it might have been, but the show as performed was a critical success. *King Kong* took Johannesburg by storm. It played in the Great Hall of the University of the Witwatersrand for a history-making multiracial audience. When the British critic Angus Wilson visited the country, the performance he saw of *King Kong* was the highlight of his trip: "The show is full of vigour and drama," he wrote. "The action takes place in a Johannesburg African township, the liveliest scene in South Africa today. Todd Matshikiza's music is the best of its kind I have heard for years. . . . The European applause was not patronage, the African applause was not partisanship, both were responding to the genuine laughs and thrills of a first-rate professional performance."[5]

Other large-scale musicals with black casts and blacks in key positions on the production teams had drawn international interest—notably *Ipi Tombi,* which had a number of successful engagements abroad, including a stand in Las Vegas, and a Zulu version of *Macbeth* called *uMabatha*—but they were aimed at white audiences, with almost no appeal to the black communities in South Africa. *King Kong,* on the other hand, had a far-reaching, cross-cultural ability to enchant. The production was a pivotal, life-transforming event for many of the people in the cast and the band—which included the most glittering South African musicians available, such as Hugh Masekela, Jonas Gwangwa, and Kippie Mokoetsie—and it motivated many other South African artists, none more directly than Kente.

With the intention of making the leap into theater work, Kente tried to commision a script from a black writer. But he failed to find one willing and available and was left with no choice but to write his own libretto and score for a play he called *Manana, the Jazz-Prophet.* He has authored every one of his productions since. Both *Manana* and his next play, *Sikalo,* were presented under the aegis of the white-run Union of South African Artists, which had produced *King Kong.* But after Kente managed to break away from the union and produce his third play himself, he began to make a name as a completely self-sufficient artist and entrepreneur, and saw to it that he never suffered the collaborative nightmares and incursions that had so bedraggled and disgusted Matshikiza. He read whatever books he could find on the subject of theater, including Konstantin Stanislavksy's writings, and applied the ideas he found where they served his needs and supported his instincts. Over the years, he developed an actor-training technique that was physically grueling and vocally exacting, in order to prepare his actors for the enormous challenge of facing off against raucous township audiences.

His productions have only rarely played outside the black locations, and then with little success. The combined effect of the broad, intense performance style, which resists modulation, and the material itself, which comes directly from the idiom and spirit of the townships, has usually hit the few white audiences who have seen his plays—leaning back in velvet-upholstered seats in a dreamy, cool, dark auditorium, hushing one another at the slightest crinkle of a candy wrapper—with a resounding thud. But for the great number of black South Africans, from the Cape to the northern Transvaal, going to see a Kente play every six months when one was in town was the only diversion from the less electrifying, less ennobling dramas of daily existence, and an important point of reference in their lives.

From 1966 to 1973, Kente created popular musical entertainments built around the experience of the township, without any political coloring, and established himself as an independent commercial force. Then he was affected by the tremendous influence of Steve Biko and Black Consciousness, and impressed by the immense international popularity of *Sizwe Banzi Is Dead* and *The Island.* His plays *How Long?, I Believe,* and *Too Late* reflected the radical spirit of the age. But in 1976, while he was adapting *How Long?* to film, he was arrested and detained under the Internal Security Act. And when he was released several months later, his post-detention play, *Can You Take It?,* showed that his prison experience had sobered him. He had been at the height of his powers before he was arrested; afterward, his plays not only rehashed old apolitical themes but lacked the thrilling artistry as well. By the time Ngema joined Kente's company in 1979 and took a leading role in *Mama and the Load,* the quality of the work had reasserted itself, but there still was lacking the heat of political relevancy.

There are some political ideas in the play I saw in 1990, but they are strikingly conservative. The auditorium at the YMCA was only half full, reflecting the current ambivalence toward Kente's newest work. Some engagements at larger halls had been canceled because of bomb threats and protests. The play is about high school students and addresses the problem of teen pregnancy, but it also communicates some reactionary ideas: In one scene, when a self-righteous boy stands up in class to sanctimoniously demand that the teacher put down the oppressors' textbook and read to them instead from their own version of history, of African kings, wars, and suffering, he is not cheered, as one might expect, but jeered by the rest of the class. Kente suggests that students should be practical instead of defiant—they should study the government's syllabus as it is. He claims that an education, regardless of its quality, is their only means for finding a place, non-violently, in the South African job market. In another scene, a student is cheated and abused by a taxi driver, and is discouraged from fighting back. Here Kente seems to be promoting the idea that boycotts and protests are irrational tactics: if you have no other way to get to school, it's best to turn the other cheek. In other recent plays, he's come out against sanctions and made fun of imperious comrades. He once told a reporter: "Political organizations are merely using people for their own ends. Necklaces, petrol bombs, and school boycotts—how do they benefit us?"

Many cultural workers in the forefront of the various anti-apartheid movements seem to be greatly troubled by Kente. Because they all grew up on his plays, it pains them to criticize him. For almost every playwright working today, even those who are the most radical and separatist in their politics, he was the earliest inspiration, and his flair, his command of the medium has been matchless. His gifts are complete: he composes the music, trains the actors, designs and builds the portable sets, which can be dismantled in under ten minutes, choreographs the dances, writes the scripts.

In spite of the occasional firebombings of his house, the threats, boycotts, and general mood of disaffection around him, Kente persists today in his own way, according to his conscience, and still has diehard fans. He vigorously pursues peace of mind and seeks out sanctuaries. He practices yoga every morning. When he decides to start a new play, he told me, he goes to Durban and takes long soulful drives along the coast. He writes the script in his car—he still drives a BMW. Kente hates tall buildings, and though the law now permits him to, he would never live in a high-rise city like Johannesburg or Durban. He prefers the townships, with their low brick shoebox houses and their unobstructed view of the sky.

In Soweto, he has been a regular and conspicuous presence at the

Orlando YMCA, a center that serves many community functions. In the gymnasium/auditorium on any afternoon, one might find a large group of small children practicing ballroom dances for semiprofessional competition, arcing and extending like swans preening themselves as they glide along the floor. In a studio next door, Kente's disciple Darlington Michaels may be drilling a group of young actors in a play of his own creation, while neighborhood children press their delighted faces up against the windows, peering in.

Kente may be in the next room, wedged between an upright piano and a wall, presiding over a cramped rehearsal with his lead actors, as he was the first time I met him. It was just a vocal rehearsal to comb out harmonies, but the actors were exerting themselves at what seemed to me to be peak performance level. They nearly burst the tiny room open. Their chests were accordions into which their necks retracted on an inhale. Their shoulders never dipped below ear level. And they filled up on air through mouths as tight and hard as inner-tube valves. Every component of their faces moved independently of the whole. A left eye narrowed while a right eyebrow hoisted itself into another, synchronous indication of meaning. They were singing in English, but it might as well have been German opera; all of the meaning was expressed in their faces and none of it in the words.

In contrast, Ngema's actors, like actors all over the world these days, have been trained to breathe into the diaphragm through an open, relaxed mouth and throat, and to leave the shoulders out of it. The voice is supported, open, and more resonant this way. Ngema's actors perform in a heightened, animated style too, but they achieve facial and physical dexterity out of a state of mastered relaxation, whereas Kente's actors seem to operate, even in a casual rehearsal, on power packs of tension. The tendons in their necks that day were tightly strung like zithers. The character of sound was, amazingly, compressed, as if passed through the neck of a demijohn, but at the same time it was booming, thunderous. Each performer seemed to sing his/her own line of harmony, contributing individually to a splendid composite richness, evocative of traditional African choral music. But Kente apparently found the sound to be painfully inadequate, for he stopped the first song in disgust and introduced another one, with a gospel flavor. Then he abruptly ended the rehearsal altogether, because he couldn't bear to have anyone hear its imperfection. "Baby," he said, in his effortless, bottomless pitch, raising a cool hand to adjust his sunglasses, one pinkie splayed, "we're going to have to stop."

▼

In the years since Ngema squatted in his garage, Kente has had to be a little more protective of his privacy. A few years ago, he attached a disclaimer to a newspaper announcement of auditions for a new play: "While I appreciate the fact that many artists over the years have made it through staying at my place, the costs these days have made it difficult for me to be able to accommodate potential artists in my house." It is fair to assume that all of the actors I saw in the rehearsal room that afternoon had originally migrated to Kente's realm as Ngema did— uninvited, inexperienced. In each of them, too, Kente detected some particular talent even before he saw them perform. Kente has been developing this gift of discernment for some thirty years.

Mary Twala has made a name for herself over the years as one of Kente's most distinguished leading ladies. In 1968, when she joined his company, she was twenty-eight years old and had been working in a galvanizing factory as the sole wage earner in her mother's house in Soweto. One weekend, she escorted her sister to the lively Johannesburg cultural center, Dorkay House, where Kente was holding auditions for his third play, *Lifa.* Twala had no intention of trying out; she spent the afternoon in the audience, dancing and clapping along with the music while her sister waited for her turn onstage. At the end of the day, however, Kente approached Twala—not her sister—and offered her a role: her unself-conscious energy had appealed to him. When she told Kente that she was reluctant to give up her job, he offered her a starting wage of 24 rand a week, three times what she'd been earning. She became, in short time, one of his most famous actresses, starring in his greatest plays and films, including *How Long?* Ndaba Mhlongo, one of Kente's most popular comedic actors, fell instantly in love with her. He wooed her with three chocolate bars a day until she finally returned his affection. Soon they were living together. By the time they married in 1972, they had become an inseparable pair—a black South African, bus-riding Nick and Nora Charles, with a shared love for theater, big laughs, boozing, and their children, all of whom are actors today. Most theatrical marriages do not last, Twala tells me, but theirs was a rock until Mhlongo's death in 1989.

Twala has come to believe that some people are simply born to be actors. She says unabashedly that the deep emotions of melodrama have always surfaced effortlessly to her face; that slapstick and eye-winking farce have come just as easily to her—as have all the possible shadings between the two extremes. Her husband was also a natural of far-reaching ability—an outrageous comedian, a sublime singer, dancer, musician.

Twala believes that Ngema, her leading man in *Mama and the Load,* was also a born actor. He adapted easily to Kente's rehearsal techniques and throve under the intensity of the process. There were long daily sessions devoted to rigorous vocal and movement training. Ngema took special interest in Kente's methods of writing and orchestrating music—in tonic sol-fa—and grilled Kente with questions.

Kente began rehearsals by demonstrating each actor's part with the desired intonation, emotion, and blocking; then he instructed the actor to duplicate his performance. He impressed modified Stanislavskyan theories of character development upon the company in order to draw from them performances that were deeper and more complex than broad caricature, but he never coaxed feeling out of them—he demanded it. Kente, indefatigable, was intolerant of actors who came to rehearsal unprepared, hadn't memorized their lines, or had forgotten what they'd learned the day before. He was known to throw fits of fury and to hurl chairs at offending actors.

After a couple of months of rehearsal, Ngema and the company boarded Kente's bus, with sets and lights in tow, and began a year-long tour of the black townships and rural homelands, stopping, as well, at the Baxter Theatre in Cape Town and the Market Theatre in Johannesburg, which were open to mixed-race audiences. Because Kente made films for state-run television—at a time when the major anti-apartheid movements condemned such involvement with the government—there were a few rough spots along the tour, where the company was not wholeheartedly welcomed; in Port Elizabeth—a city that has always generated sophisticated political activism—they were run out of town.

The actors endured many difficulties during the long tour. Kente failed to pay his company regularly; to protest, the actors refused to perform until they were compensated. When they resumed the tour, they played one-night stands along a course that covered a large and exhausting country, with pockets of nauseating heat, jagged mountain passes, and unpaved township roads. Day in, day out, they traveled in a rickety, unreliable bus overcrowded with tricky artistic personalities. The stress led to a good deal of debauchery and drinking, and the consequent gloom of hangovers. Most of the company slept on the hard wooden benches on the bus—Twala and Mhlongo had spent the better part of their nights as a married couple curled up on neighboring seats. Ngema and a singer in the chorus, Percy Mtwa, who had become his close friend, made a vow not to fall in love with women in the company, because if they did, they, too, would always have to sleep on the bus. The women they met in the towns they visited enabled them to escape briefly from this stifling confinement. They left girlfriends behind in almost every stop on the tour.

It was during the long bus rides that Ngema and Mtwa began the deep discourses that led to *Woza Albert!* A fellow actor in the company found a copy of Jerzy Grotowski's manifesto, *Towards a Poor Theatre,* and passed it on to them. As they pored over the book, fantastic phrases floated up at them: "We consider the personal and scenic technique of the actor as the core of theater art," Grotowski writes.[6] "Impulse and action are concurrent. . . ." "I propose poverty in theater. . . ." He defines the "holy actor" as one who, "through his art, climbs upon the stake and performs an act of self-sacrifice." To their surprise, Ngema and Mtwa discovered that they met every one of Grotowski's criteria for the holy actor. Kente, like Grotowski, had demanded unhesitating impulse and action. Were there poorer actors, working under more arduous conditions, anywhere in the world?

In a series of articles within the book, written by Grotowski himself and others in his company, details of training exercises—designed to prepare the actor for concurrence in impulse and action—are delineated. There are meticulous calisthenic workouts for the fingers, the eyeballs, the voice, and all-involving exercises such as one in which two students enact the lovemaking of animals, employing the voice and the whole body with abandon. There are yoga and relaxation exercises. There is also the "tiger" exercise, in which, in his own laboratory in Poland, Grotowski would play the tiger attacking his prey. "I'm going to eat you," he would menace. "It was remarkable," the narrator writes, "how the pupils were carried away by the exercise."

Ngema and Mtwa also experimented with transcendental meditation as a countermeasure to the disquiet of the bus, and read the Bible from cover to cover. They debated the parables and proposed scenarios, some hilarious, some stinging, of the second coming set in South Africa: What would Jesus say when he saw apartheid? What would South Africans ask of him? Would he arrive by airplane? They became excited about collaborating on a play that would adapt Grotowski's concepts to their own ideas inspired by the New Testament. Weary of the constant traveling and eager to address themselves fully to their own project, they secretly planned to leave Kente. Twala, who was in charge of the cash box, remembers that after about a year on the road, Ngema and Mtwa woke her on the bus in the middle of the night somewhere near Durban and asked for 7 rand each. In the morning, they had disappeared. The remaining schedule had to be canceled, for no one was prepared to take over Ngema's principal role. But for the most part, the company was happy to put an end to the prolonged tour and return to Johannesburg.

Ngema took Mtwa to Khassi and Bongi's house in Umlazi. In the yard, beneath the avocado tree, they experimented with Grotowski's exercises and began to consider their work in a new light: "The acceptance of poverty in theater," writes Grotowski, "stripped of all that is not essential to it, revealed to us not only the backbone of the medium, but also the deep riches which lie in the very nature of the art-form." Ngema heard echoes of the first play he'd ever seen, *Sizwe Banzi*, in which a character proclaims, "this world leaves us nothing, except ourselves." Suddenly, seen in the light of this outsider's vision, oneself did not seem at all like nothing. Oneself, in the theater of Grotowski, was everything.

Khassi often sat in the shade of the tree with his bottle of brandy and watched as they improvised the new play. They intended to call it

Our Father Who Art in Heaven and planned for a large cast of seven actors. For the time being, they had to play all the roles themselves, and wholly transformed themselves for each new scene they sketched out. The economy of their "poor theater" was a matter of necessity, not of choice. But they came to regard themselves in Grotowski's exalted light, as "holy" actors whose job it was to climb upon the stake.

They found further fuel for their exhilaration in another book they discovered at this time, *The Empty Space* by Peter Brook, who, like Grotowski, regarded Antonin Artaud as a preeminent prophet of the theater. During a break from their work in Khassi's backyard, they read the first line of the book: "I can take any empty space and call it a bare stage. A man walks across this empty space whilst someone else is watching him, and this is all that is needed for an act of theater to be engaged."[7]

"I am calling it the Holy Theatre for short," Brook writes further on, "but it could be called The Theatre of the Invisible-Made-Visible: the notion that the stage is a place where the invisible can appear has a deep hold on our thoughts." During long, philosophical, drunken symposia and debates in the yard, Ngema and Mtwa outlined an ambitious plan for a cultural center that could be a laboratory for their play and a school where they could teach others what they'd been teaching themselves. *The Empty Space* substantiated this idea, saying: "It must also be faced that even a permanent company is doomed to deadliness in the long run if it is without an aim, and thus without a method, and thus without a school."

But determination wouldn't be enough to bring their dreams to life. Although he had worked steadily for a year, Ngema was as down and out as he had ever been, with no means to implement his plans. Furthermore, the townships, as always, were engulfed in crisis. Ngema had always been able to lock the front door of his mind against the chaos and indignity of violence and poverty, while opening the back door to a garden of "vaguely felt notions" of art and beauty, but this required a rare aptitude for confidence and concentration. Who else in this place would have the time or tranquillity to learn eyeball exercises and "holy theater" from two bohemian wanderers?

CHAPTER SIX

▼

What was it that made me conscious of possibilities? From where in this southern darkness had I caught a sense of freedom? Why was it that I was able to act upon vaguely felt notions? What was it that made me feel things deeply enough for me to try to reorder my life by my feelings?

RICHARD WRIGHT,
Black Boy[1]

In 1976, the South African government conferred sovereign independence upon the Transkei, a Xhosa homeland. But neither the United Nations nor the Organization of African Unity nor any polity or group in the world, with the exception of the International Tug-of-War Federation,[2] recognized it. Most black South Africans, inside and outside the Transkei, opposed independence, which was widely perceived as a sham: a major step toward the apartheid engineers' long-term goal of "separate development"—or divide and rule—of the black majority. After 1976, the homeland's economy was still tightly controlled from Pretoria, and its population still served as a labor reservoir for white businesses beyond its borders. Most of the blacks who supported independence were elite businesspeople and corrupt Transkeian chiefs and politicians, dominated by Kaiser (K.D.) Matanzima and his younger brother, George.

During the period of transition to independence, however, when Pretoria slackened its ties, the Matanzimas and the Transkeian legislative assembly achieved at least one positive advancement for their people—they abolished Bantu Education, adopted a European-style syllabus, and oversaw a tremendous expansion of the teaching establishment. When they toured with Kente's company in Umtata, the homeland's capital, Ngema and Mtwa found a novel, educated refinement among the people they met. Later, they thought it might be just the place for their cultural center and drama school.

Ngema left Mtwa in Umlazi and traveled alone to Umtata in order to make the necessary contacts and preparations. By now Ngema had learned that if he exercised a little determination and charm, no potentate was out of his reach. Shortly after his arrival, he succeeded in arranging a meeting with the reigning prime minister, George Matanzima, whose older brother had removed himself to a slightly less accountable post. A driver in a Mercedes came to fetch Ngema and delivered him to the capitol, where security was lax. Ngema was directed to walk directly into George's office, which he found empty. Then the driver transported him to George's official residence, a modern castle staffed with an army of servants. Ngema waited on a velvet sofa in the parlor for only ten or fifteen minutes before he was joined by George, who listened intently and responded enthusiastically to Ngema's proposal. At parting, George promised that he would consider the cultural center further and contact Ngema shortly with a formal response. Although George was more commonly recognized for his political depravity and material greed, those who knew him personally often said that he had a sympathetic heart.

But George was surely not feeling as secure as he seemed. In the year or so preceding his meeting with Ngema, the opposition to his government had consolidated and intensified. There had been rumors of a germinating coup. Thousands of subversive pamphlets had been distributed throughout the homeland, labeling the Matanzimas as puppets of the apartheid regime, who fleeced their citizenry and used coercive means to extract and confer wealth. Many an Umtata housewife, it was widely held, secured business licenses by offering herself to K.D., who favored married women. George was reputed to be a pedophile.

After the declaration of independence, the Transkeian legislature inherited a good number of internal security acts from South Africa, which were useful at times like these. Detention without trial, arrest without warrant, banning of people and organizations, limitations to freedom of speech when it was hostile to the government or contemptuous of independence, were all provided for, and the maximum penalty for seditious acts or expressions was death. In June 1980, immediately after he was visited by Ngema, George declared a state of emergency and clamped down on his opposition. Undermining the dignity of the state president was made a capital charge.

On the basis of the promising meeting with George, Mtwa soon joined Ngema, and they settled in Umtata with great optimism, innocent of any danger. They stayed with a young man in iKhwezi, a residential location near the main business district, and pursued their Grotowskian laboratory work and their improvisations, while awaiting a green light from the government. Gradually, they assembled a thick, handwritten script, which they guarded obsessively.

▼

On the bus ride from Durban to Umtata, Ngema had met a Transkeian woman named Thembela, with whom he'd shared an instantaneous magnetic attraction. Returning home from a visit to her mother, who was a domestic worker in KwaZulu, Thembela had her four-year-old daughter seated beside her. Ngema had noticed that a man had escorted Thembela onto the bus. But he approached her anyway, and was pleased to learn that the man was only a friend. She had two daughters but had never been married. Satisfied that his future with Thembela was rosy, he asked her if she'd excuse him for a few minutes while he returned to his seat to finish a chapter in the book he was reading. Thembela was flustered by Ngema's interest and his politeness—his characteristically attentive Zulu respect. When he came back to her, he made a formal romantic proposition. On the most direct course, the journey from Durban to Umtata takes less than three hours. But because of the many stops on this route, their ride lasted twelve hours. By the time they arrived in Umtata—Thembela was continuing on to Port St. Johns, where she lived—they had become well acquainted. They met again a few weeks later and became lovers. And Thembela became Ngema's—and Mtwa's—sole source of income. She began to contribute half of her monthly salary of 125 rand. With the other half, she somehow managed to support her family.

Thembela's previous relationship—with the father of her two daughters—was extremely unhappy. An irresponsible man, unemployed, perfidious, he had seriously mangled her self-esteem. She was left feeling plain and ordinary in every way, and because she had two children, she doubted that anyone would ever want to marry her. From the onset of her affair with Ngema, she assumed that she would never merit a marriage proposal from him, but she was happy with him. He found her lovely and told her so convincingly. Thembela took advantage of her position as a telephone operator in Port St. Johns—though she thereby risked her job—to phone Ngema almost every day. Though she was able to visit him in Umtata only a few times during his residence there, she remembers vividly watching Ngema and Mtwa rehearsing their play, practicing exercises that seemed ridiculous to her, provoking her laughter. Mtwa didn't seem to like her much, but when the work was finished, Ngema would hold Thembela on his lap, and they would all sing amiably.

More frequently, Ngema would visit Thembela in Port St. Johns, a secluded, restful ocean resort that attracted white vacationers, especially those who liked to fish. There were no private *kombitaxis* in those days, only public buses, and the road was rough, so the journey took a long time. First the bus rolled through standard farmland, densely settled with livestock and mud rondavels. Then it crept gradually up into more drastically sloping, sparsely populated mountain terrain accented by high peaks of gray rock; and still farther up to ear-popping heights. Occasionally one could catch a glimpse of a tilted, gravity-defying kraal carved into the rocks. Suddenly a magnificent unpeopled vista unfurled as the bus tiptoed along the apogee of the Mlengana mountain range. Then began the slow descent toward the sea. The unpaved road passed through slightly more habitable terrain, where pigs and goats asserted themselves against the pitch of the landscape and women balanced oversize loads on their heads, seemingly against the laws of physics. Children ran at a slant toward the bus, waving up at the riders. The road wound and dipped and switched back and lurched. The bus swayed along a sheer drop, then swung and looped down and passed through a tract of hushed, cool, cultivated forest. And then, at last, over a wall of rock, Ngema could catch a glimpse of the sea. Enormous trees bent over the road as the bus coasted to the rugged shore, dark rock, white sea, the constant movement of air and water that distinguished Port St. Johns.

Ngema loved Thembela. But they were separated for considerable periods of time, and she wasn't the only woman in his life. Umtata, Ngema says, was filled with beautiful, flirtatious women who, he eventually discovered, were actually government spies. "They'd take us to parties," he says, "and because we had nothing in our pockets and needed their help, we'd end up telling them what we were about." One woman in particular was very solicitous and excessively kind, and she offered to type up their script for them. She took the sole handwritten copy and promised to return with it in a few days. When she finally came back, however, she had a terrible announcement to make: She had been mugged in Ngangelizwe by thugs who ran off with the script.

The houses in Ngangelizwe, a very old, poor urban township with no electricity, were not the typical rectangular brick boxes built to code but mostly antediluvian mud structures, both round and square, with all manner of thatched and corrugated roofs, weighted down by boulders and huge pieces of furniture—a bureau, a desk, the shell of a piano. Their exteriors were painted endlessly varying cheerful shades of pink, blue, green, lavender, yellow. The houses leaned and billowed, slouched and sank, for blocks and blocks, suggesting a multicolored ghetto in the forest of Hansel and Gretel. With throbbing hearts, Ngema and Mtwa searched among blue houses shaped like mushrooms, pink houses like lopsided marshmallows, and yellow rondavels that had been plastered and replastered, painted and repainted, for untold generations. They followed laundry lines that crossed from one structure to another, threading every loop and hook of the township like a sewing machine. They desperately hoped to catch sight of the pages of the script blowing around a corner, or to find even a single page stuck to the bottom of one of their shoes. Maybe the thugs had dropped the parcel in disinterest! For three consecutive days, they returned to Ngangelizwe, but they never found the script because it wasn't there.

When they abandoned their search, they relocated to the township of Norwood, where they'd been invited to stay with a friend whose mother was one of Umtata's leading retailers. She loaned Ngema and Mtwa a typewriter, which they used to begin to reassemble their script from scratch, laboriously, one stroke at a time. When they returned to iKhwezi to visit their friends, they were told that the police had been looking for them. They thought nothing of it. Returning a day or two later, they were told that the police had again been looking for them, and Ngema and Mtwa unsuspectingly decided to visit the police station to find out what they wanted. Strangely, they saw just outside the station many of the pretty women they'd met since they'd arrived in the Transkei.

As soon as they presented themselves before the police, Ngema and Mtwa were detained as terrorists and thrown into solitary confinement in two separate prisons, with no trial or bail set. Later that day, their friend in Norwood was arrested as an accessory. The woman "typist," they came to understand, worked for the government and had handed their script over to the secret police. The play was loosely structured around stories from the New Testament in the spirit of Grotowski and Brook. In later versions, the work did adopt a sharp political attitude, but the first draft had nothing whatever to do with the Matanzimas or the Transkei. The local police, however, were suspicious of every printed word and wary of double meanings and subversive messages hidden between the lines of any document, no matter how innocuous it appeared to be.

While in confinement, Ngema used the Bible in his cell to continue his research, and he kept a cool head by pursuing his regime of vocal and physical exercises. He was eventually displaced from his solitary chamber by a more threatening criminal and moved to a crowded cell down the hall from an interrogation room where acts of South African–style torture and coercion were performed. Still, he performed his exercises in the presence of other prisoners, with one of

Boys eating leftovers at a recent Ngema family feast, Hlabisa. (*Laura Jones*)

Men enjoying the best parts of the beast in a segregated enclosure. (*Laura Jones*)

Thandi Zulu at her
home in Umlazi, 1990.
(*Laura Jones*)

Margaret at her
Umlazi retirement
home, 1990.
(*Laura Jones*)

Sam and his wife in front of their shop, 1991. (*Laura Jones*)

Khassi and Bongi outside their home, 1990.
(*Laura Jones*)

A publicity photo (session funded by Khassi) for *Too Harsh*; Ngema pictured here with Mafiki.

Mary Twala in mourning, shortly after the death of her husband, Ndaba Mhlongo. Orlando, Soweto, 1990. (*Laura Jones*)

Thembela, during a visit to Johannesburg in 1990. (*Laura Jones*)

Ngema poses with Ignatia, seen here with some of the children in her care. Standing at rear, Ngema's brother Siyoni Mdletshe. Pimville, 1991. (*Laura Jones*)

Ngema and Percy Mtwa in the Market Theatre production of *Woza Albert!*
(© *Ruphin Coudyzer*)

Asinamali! (© *Pam Frank*)

Leleti Khumalo, at center, in the finale of *Sarafina!* (© 1987 *Brigitte Lacombe*)

Sheila Paris hosting a party for the *Township Fever* cast in her Harlem apartment, 1991. *(Laura Jones)*

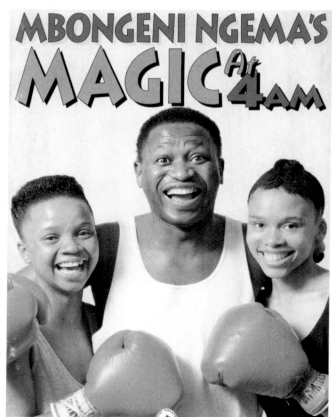

From the program for the Johannesburg Civic Theatre production of *Magic at 4 A.M.*: Seipati Sothoane, Bhoyi Ngema, and Leleti Khumalo. (© 1993 *Thomas Khosa*)

whom, Hector Ncokazi, he became especially friendly. One of the most intractable adversaries of the Matanzimas, Ncokazi had been in detention steadily since "independence." "Someday the hunters will become the hunted," he assured Ngema, who with every passing day found his situation more detestable. In the meantime, Ncokazi suggested that Ngema write a letter to George Matanzima; perhaps he'd remember their meeting and show mercy. "I appeal to you because you are the man who knows why I am here," Ngema wrote.

A week and a half later, after thirty-three days in prison, Ngema and Mtwa were escorted to the nearest train station and deported with no explanation. When they were asked where they intended to go, they decided on Johannesburg. They were sharply admonished to vacate the Transkei before nightfall, but neither Ngema nor Mtwa had money for train tickets. So Ngema called Thembela, collect, and told her that he urgently needed cash. She borrowed the sum from co-workers and wired it to the Umtata post office that afternoon.

Ngema's call came as a relief to Thembela. When he had been detained, his daily calls had suddenly stopped. For two weeks, she'd worried terribly, until finally he'd managed to get to a phone in prison and called her, begging her to visit him. The next Sunday morning, she took the bus up away from the sea, across the Mlengana Mountains, and down into Umtata; then another bus to the prison. But the first bus had been delayed, and she arrived too late to get in to see him or even to send a message. "Oh, did I cry," she says. "I wondered why I was crying: 'Why am I crying? Mbongeni is not dead. But I'm sure he needs me.' I knew he would feel hurt." She had to return immediately to Port St. Johns in order to be on time for work in the morning, and she wept the whole way home. "That's one of the days that I thought: Oh, I feel deeply about this man." The next time she heard from him was two weeks later, when he called from the train station for money.

▼

From Johannesburg, Ngema and Mtwa proceeded to Daveyton, a black township forty-five minutes east of the city, where Mtwa's family lived. Thembela was still their only source of income, and she continued to wire them money. Their poverty caused persistent anxiety and discord. If Thembela's offering was the slightest bit late in arriving, Mtwa would complain to Ngema. Then Ngema would snap at Mtwa: "Why can't *you* get a girlfriend who will send money!?" Then Ngema would call Thembela and castigate her: "Why didn't you send me money! How do you think I'm going to eat!" Ashamed afterward, he would apologize profusely. Thembela would send the money, which would quickly ooze away. It was an ugly, debasing experience. This man who had played in Gibson Kente's company and been acclaimed and feted in every township *still* had days when he dined on nothing but dry bread. He was still surprising friends with unexpected lunch-time appearances at their homes.

From their monthly allowance, Ngema and Mtwa allocated a small sum of cash for a fee enabling them to use the facilities at FUBA, an arts school for black students in the city of Johannesburg, where they began rehearsing daily. Ngema had one outfit of clothing, a cream-colored track suit, which he wore every day and washed every night. When he discovered that an *inyanga* (a traditional healer) he knew from Durban was living in Johannesburg, he and Mtwa began jogging to the man's shop every day at noon; there they would receive a meal. The *inyanga,* a very spiritual man, believed in Ngema. "That shirt," he'd say to him; "I like it very much. But one day, you will have money, and then I want to see that shirt. The man who wears this shirt must never change."

A month after their arrival in Daveyton, Ngema and Mtwa were kicked out of Mtwa's brother's house. They split up and sponged off whomever they could, meeting every day to rehearse at FUBA. One day, Mtwa failed to show up for rehearsal, and Ngema wandered into the music department, picked up a guitar, and started playing. In distinctive Zulu-style guitar, each string contributes an independent line of melody to create an overlapping sound, nearly impossible to transpose. A fellow down the hall heard the music, walked into the room, and said, "Hey, you play like you come from Durban, like me." Ngema told the man the long story of his ambitions as a theater artist and how he had no place to sleep and nothing to his name but the track suit he was wearing. The man said that he was staying with a widow and her children in Pimville, one of the older townships in Soweto. She was an old-age pensioner, but she was very generous, he said, and would certainly welcome Ngema too.

Her name was Ignatia. She was a good Catholic woman with the standard four-room house and the average seventeen to twenty children sleeping on sofas, in Ignatia's bed, and on the floor. Once she juggled her family about, there was even a place for Ngema to sleep. A day or two later, Ngema found Mtwa at FUBA and took him back to Pimville. And Ignatia made one more small place. The four walls never gave or budged, but they did not limit her in the least. There seemed to be no end to the number of bunks, berths, and sacks she could accommodate. Very often, in the middle of the night, the precarious arrangement was shattered into chaos by police conducting a random raid. Ngema would hear a distant pounding and the barking of dogs; he would feel the lambent heat of a flashlight in his face; then came pandemonium. The lodgers would tumble from their beds, their hearts pounding. Ignatia would shriek, the children would wail. But the next day, the old woman would miraculously restore order and balance to the household.

Though very poor, Ignatia knew how to feed her family, how to make visitors feel welcome, and how to have pleasure. She was slowed down physically by the cumbersome bosom that most South African women seem to accrue, beginning at a very young age, which no brassieres are made to fit. Her legs were swollen from a lifetime of excessive standing and walking—she probably had never had an opportunity to sit with her feet raised to promote circulation. She was without a husband. She cared for her children, her children's children, her nieces and nephews, and the children of friends. She was uneducated and spoke no useful English. All of the household money went toward food and school fees. She wore remnants of old dresses and aprons layered upon each other, pinned at the seams. She lived in a terribly distressed area within Soweto. And yet she hadn't lost her goodwill or her talent for enjoyment. Thembela came to visit for three weeks and had the most lighthearted, romantic time that she would ever spend with Ngema. Ignatia honored her by calling her *makoti* (daughter-in-law).

▼

Although Ngema and Mtwa had planned on a large cast in their play, they'd accepted now that it would be only the two of them. For seven months they rehearsed at FUBA, mastering all of Grotowski's exercises and training themselves into terrific physical condition by jogging daily from Pimville to town.

At the Market Theatre in Johannesburg some time earlier, they'd seen *Call Me Woman,* a play that Barney Simon, the Market's artistic director, had created with a company of black actresses. Originally, Simon had expected to mount American playwright/poet Ntozake Shange's play *For Colored Girls Who Have Considered Suicide/When the Rainbow Is Enuf,* but the rights were withdrawn at the last moment. So he worked with the company to write their own play, thematically related to Shange's, through improvisation and collective research. Ngema and Mtwa admired the production and decided that they'd like to work with Simon someday. When they heard that the Market was holding open auditions for the upcoming season, they offered themselves as actors. They did not make a strong impression on the managing director, Mannie Manim, who oversaw the auditions—he remembers that their performances were rather terrible—but they took the opportunity to tell him about their own play, and a couple of months later they persuaded him to let them exhibit the work.

In a rehearsal room, before a group of Market associates and friends, including Barney Simon, they presented their first act, which ran a good two hours. The script rambled, but the fantastic energy of the actors and the brilliance of their physical transformations overwhelmed the audience (later, a critic in Los Angeles would call it an "unquenchable life force"). Ngema and Mtwa were ecstatic when the run-through was over. After seven months of research and improvisation, and all their drills and dramatic calisthenics in Johannesburg, following several months in Durban and the Transkei, they'd finally shown their work. And the response was even better than they'd hoped for. Afterward, Manim told them to choose carefully the director they'd like to work with. They accepted the gravity of the decision, stepped out of Manim's office for a moment, and went directly back and said, "We want Barney Simon."

Simon was not only Manim's administrative partner but an extremely busy working director. Assuming that they'd make an alternative choice, Manim informed them that Simon was already engaged; they'd have to wait two months if they wanted him. They said, "Fine, we'll wait." Two months later, they returned. Manim told them they'd have to wait three additional weeks for Simon. Ngema and Mtwa said, "Fine; we'll come back."

Simon was reluctant to become involved at this point. Recently, he'd had some painful experiences with black playwrights and actors—with whom he'd once collaborated splendidly—who had suddenly announced that they would no longer work with him, or any other white, on political and moral principles. Simon had learned to enter into all new professional relationships with guarded apprehension. When Ngema and Mtwa returned again to the Market, Simon gave them a list of black directors, but finally he accepted the job himself. He found the script to be in need of major renovation, but he was enthralled by the physical metamorphoses the actors underwent to play the many characters in their scenario, with no costumes, sets, or lights to enhance the illusion. This form—the "poor theater" that Ngema and Mtwa had arrived at out of necessity, proclivity, and circumstance—was exactly the kind of work Simon had been moving toward for many years.

Chapter Seven

▼

What we need's a new kind of theater. New forms are what we need, and if we haven't got them we'd be a sight better off with nothing at all.

Treplev
in *The Cherry Orchard,*
by ANTON CHEKHOV[1]

*Was it worth it? Everything is worthwhile
If the soul is not mean.*

FERNANDO PESSOA[2]

"If there's anything that's fundamental to my work," Barney Simon says, "it's reading Braque the painter saying that he began to understand the nature of art during the First World War when he saw a soldier take a bucket that had carried water, punch holes into it, and transform it into a brazier to carry fire. It's that potential for metamorphosis in all things that art should express."

Simon has brought about no transformation more dazzling than the one through which he and Mannie Manim and their associates recast the shell of Johannesburg's old Indian Fruit Market into the theater that it is today, a center of humming activity, generating light and heat. Constructed in 1916 in the Newtown section of the city, the market operated for nearly sixty years as it was initially intended. "This market is one place where I like to be," wrote Dugmore Boetie, a gangster who'd frequented the original market in its heyday and described it in his autobiography.³ "I could wander about it the whole day and never get tired or bored with it. The fruit stalls with their crafty-looking owners, their high-pitched voices forever urging passersby to examine and buy their fruit. This place is a symbol of life, guile and greed." To lure housewives into the disreputable neighborhood where the market was located, there were tram rides, brass bands, and, on Sundays, symphony concerts in the main hall.

In the most inauspicious year imaginable, 1976—the year of the student uprisings, of the hotly contested Transkeian independence, of a major economic slump, of the advent of television to bewitch South Africans and hold them captive—Simon and Manim, along with a group of actors called The Company and an adventurous board of trustees, transformed the Indian Fruit Market into the Market Theatre. "The idea of getting decent people to go there at night is so stupid I would spend money to stop you," one businessman who declined to make a donation reportedly said. Today the Indian hawkers and the brass band are gone, but the surrounding neighborhood is still disreputable; many of the original signboards and accoutrements of the old market remain as decorations, and the reincarnated Market is more than ever a place where one may spend the entire day and never get bored. The street that the theater faces has been turned into an outdoor mall, with restaurants in all price ranges, a jazz club, a cabaret, FUBA, numerous workshops and studios, a bookstore, a flower market, an African arts-and-crafts store, and other shops in a connected arcade. Within the flagship theater building itself there's a pub, a snack bar (open all day), three performance spaces, two art galleries, and another bookstore.

If you're looking for a particular musician, actor, playwright, journalist, or artist, there is a good chance you'll find him somewhere in the Market mall, or at least find someone who can tell you when he was last seen and when he's expected to return. There is also a faction of unemployed black actors and directors who dress up every morning and take taxis in from Soweto or crosstown from Hillbrow just to mill about in the pleasant afternoon sun, prolong the life of a cup of coffee for hours, and socialize with their peers. Cries of *"Howzzit umfowethu!"* (Whassup, brother) and "Sharp, sharp!" ricochet across the mall all day. I asked a young actor who had been expelled from the original cast of *Sarafina!* for irresponsible behavior while the company was in New York, and who hadn't worked since, why he could always be found in the mall. He told me, "I'm a man of the theater, baby—where else should I be?" Later, I learned that he was squatting in an abandoned warehouse nearby and taking his daily showers in the theater's men's dressing room.

▼

The *New York Times* journalist Joseph Lelyveld has remarked that the "Market Theatre operates as if it had some extraterrestrial status, making it immune to the country's racial and censorship laws."[4] Most of the supporting structure of those laws were removed—like a plaster mold—in the last few years, but the apartheid conformation, like hardened bronze, still continued to hold. The Market has always existed as a kind of free zone in the center of relentless urban warfare. Most of the programming and business decisions over the years have been overseen by Manim and Simon, who are white, but there are many black people (meaning Indians, people of mixed race, and Africans) in general and house management positions, and many more working as ushers, bartenders, box office clerks, stagehands, and housekeepers. The pool of creative personnel seems to reflect, on most days, the racial demographics of the country at large. In no place but South Africa could one make such distinctions politely, but make no mistake: what has been achieved at the Market would be considered a miracle in any major modern city in America or Europe. I know of no institutional theater in New York City or, for that matter, any regional theater in America that has managed to epitomize and employ the diverse constituencies of the cities they inhabit with the degree of success, consistency, and unselfconsciousness of the Market Theatre.

A good number of black writers and directors—John Ledwaba, Maishe Maponya, and Matsemela Manaka, to name a few—have worked more or less regularly at the Market over the years, attracting multiracial audiences and foreign producers who have moved some of their productions overseas. I was in the country during *Township Fever*'s 1990 run at the Market; on most nights, as I'm told it has been with all of Ngema's productions, the main arena looked nearly as black as Soweto, where most in the audience had come from by bus or *kombi*. Ngema always writes his texts in English, but he peppers them with inside jokes in the vernacular languages and idioms, which are incomprehensible to most of the white people who do come to see the show. (When the play moves overseas, those jokes are usually excised.) Ngema depicts harsh realities in his works, but like Kente, he aims above all to entertain. The black audiences tend to crack up at a comedic line and then dissolve just as readily into moans and wails during a heart-wrenching speech or song, the strongest of which will also be in the vernacular. When Afrikaans was the official national language and English the language of writers and of speechmakers like Nelson Mandela, the popular music and theater of the day demonstrated that the vernacular languages were still the vehicles of feeling in South Africa. "A people may have its language taken away from it," wrote T. S. Eliot, "suppressed, and another language compelled upon the schools; but unless you teach that people to *feel* in a new language, you have not eradicated the old one."[5]

The Babel-like nature of South Africa makes the Market's heterogeneity seem even more remarkable. At intermission and after the performances, the multilingual audiences empty from the various venues into the center of the mall, where they chat and sip coffee beneath the stars.

▼

Barney Simon has done his principal work in the South African theater, but he has also seen a good deal of the world and has worked as a magazine editor, short-story writer, film director, and health educator. He has acquired a broad-based, even-tempered epistemology and philosophy. He served his apprenticeship in the London theater of renegade director Joan Littlewood, whom the British critic Kenneth Tynan once described as "some latter-day William Blake let loose on show business," and was deeply, lastingly affected by the experience. Tynan wrote: "Joan is a missionary whose aim is the total destruction of complacent, well-behaved middle-class theater." She founded her company, the Theatre Workshop, in 1945, with the immediate ambition of creating a "Leftist living newspaper presenting instant dramatizations of contemporary history."[6] She was contemptuous of the West End and founded her company in Manchester. But many of her productions—such as *Oh, What a Lovely War!,* a satirical encapsulation of World War I, which eventually played on Broadway—were so popular that she couldn't prevent them from moving to the big commercial houses in London. The Living Newspaper concept and Littlewood's use of improvisation became important tools in Simon's own later work.

Simon returned to South Africa, where he began his career in 1961 in the immediate aftermath of a watershed in modern South African history, the Sharpeville Massacre, during which 67 blacks protesting peacefully against the country's pass laws were killed by police and another 186 were wounded, most of them shot in the back. Subsequently the government banned the African National Congress and the Pan-Africanist Congress and declared a state of emergency. Simon worked with Athol Fugard at Dorkay House in Johannesburg, where Fugard's earliest theater experiments, *No Good Friday* and *Nongogo,* had been improvised and scripted with black casts. When in the turmoil of the sixties the government effectively shut them down, Fugard went home to the Eastern Cape to pursue his theater work. Simon, however, subsidized by the salary he earned as an advertising copywriter, rented a room in a condemned mansion in a Johannesburg suburb for 8 rand a month and invited private audiences to see the productions he staged there of avant-garde plays, including Jean Genet's *The Maids.*

In 1968, he went to New York and met the photographer Bruce Davidson, who was compiling a book about the Young Lords, "a Puerto Rican counterpart to the Black Panthers," as Simon puts it, who were presenting socially relevant theater in abandoned warehouses in East Harlem. He spent some time, too, around Joseph Chaikin, who also employed a workshop approach in constructing plays with the company he founded in 1964, the Open Theatre.

When Simon returned to South Africa, he started a roving company called Mirror One and created work inspired by what he'd seen in New York. His company performed in Johannesburg living rooms and backyards—they once performed in a garden for the sole benefit of the man confined next door under house arrest.

Later, Simon went to work for the state-subsidized Performing Arts Council of the Transvaal (PACT) as a director. He also ran workshops at mission hospitals in Zululand and the Transkei, guiding nurses in the creation of didactic songs and dramatic enactments that communicated essential health-care precepts in the vernacular, often performed in open fields. "Remember the words of Shaka: the size of a man's field must depend on his ability to irrigate; have as many children as you can feed, clothe, and educate," went the lyrics to one of the songs (Simon's translation). And another: "Never give your child an enema when he has diarrhea. What shall I do? Take him off solid foods, give him a little salt water, and if it continues, bring him to the doctor." (Doctors who minister to blacks are scarce throughout the country, in the urban centers as well as the rural areas. But traditional herbal healers—*inyangas*—and spiritualists are ubiquitous and tend to prescribe organic enemas, emetics, and laxatives as purifying remedies for every imaginable ailment, including broken bones and broken hearts.) The lyrics were sung to compelling melodies and harmonies.

The work with the nurses was a critical experience in Simon's life, dominating a period of time when many ideas and revelations sneaked up on him, very often while he was driving between Johannesburg and Zululand or down the rough coast to his workshops in the Transkei. Physically, South Africa is so spectacularly beautiful, so soul-stirring, so large and enlarging, that if it were even many degrees less beautiful it would still be ostentatious. Today there is lots of good, smooth open road—the kind of road Walt Whitman would have loved. In some places, especially along high-speed trucking routes through mountain ranges, the driving can be extremely hazardous. But if one has peace of mind and no distractions, one may inhale great drafts of space while driving, conceive heroic deeds, and reexamine philosophies learned in school. Many South African writers and artists have told me that their best ideas, their illuminating moments, have come to them on the road.

Mannie Manim, Simon's eventual partner in the Market Theatre enterprise, says that about twenty years ago, after ten years in the service of complacent, well-behaved, middle-class theater, he turned his entire life around during an extensive road trip that crossed the whole expanse of the country.

When Manim was seven years old, his father died, leaving the family destitute. Subsequently, his mother moved them from their home in the Cape to a poor white area of Johannesburg called Jeppe. Manim decided at an early age that he wanted to become a bridge-builder when he grew up. But at the age of fifteen he got an after-school job as an usher and stagehand for an actor-manager named Brian Brooke, who specialized in productions of American musicals like *Irma La Douce* and *The Pajama Game.* Brooke's staff became Manim's extended family. The experience revised his concept of the future, starting him on a trajectory through most of the commercial theaters that opened and closed over the years in Johannesburg.

One Sunday night, Athol Fugard's play *No Good Friday* and its cast of sophisticated, now legendary, black writers and actors—Bloke Modisane, Lewis Nkosi, Zakes Mokae, Nat Nakasa—borrowed the Brooke Theatre for a single performance. Manim remembers the alien thrill he felt when he heard the company conferring in the vernacular backstage in the smoking area, in contrast to the elegant English they spoke onstage, but he had no further contact with either Fugard or any black artists for many years. He worked behind the scenes on productions of American musicals, occasionally a Tennessee Williams or a Harold Pinter play, and, rarely, an original white South African play.

Manim developed expertise in the technical zones of the profession. At the country's first state theater, the Civic, he stage-managed an enormous production of *Showboat,* which featured actual flowing water onstage. He devised a way for the boat to contract like a concertina at the farthest point upstage and then unfold with actors on three decks, giving the effect of rolling down the river toward the audience. He oversaw guest performances by international artists—including Danny Kaye and Christopher Hewett, the actor who appeared as the title character on "Mr. Belvedere," the American TV sitcom. Hewett starred in *A Funny Thing Happened on the Way to the Forum* at the Civic and taught Manim about how Broadway and West End rehearsals are run.

Manim managed tours to Australia and across Africa. He encountered a remarkable company called Eon, comprising a group of mixed-race singers from Cape Town who sang impeccable Italian opera. He learned to design lights, a specialty for which he is highly respected and perpetually sought after today.

In 1971, Manim went to work for PACT, where he came to know Simon and Fugard. In his new administrative position, he developed an interest in taking shows to black audiences, who were prohibited by law from attending the white theaters. He hired American director Charles Marowitz to direct *Macbeth* with white South African actors and persuaded the council to let him tour the show through the townships. This was an enormously successful and gratifying experience for Manim. But his pivotal moment of truth came when a group of Black Consciousness–minded Indians refused to allow the show to perform in Lenasia, an Indian community in the Johannesburg area, because of the production's connection to PACT and consequently to the state. The rejection hurt Manim personally and provoked him to reevaluate his life. He set out on a three-month-long drive from the northernmost point of the country down to Cape Town, stopping along the way in Port Elizabeth to see Fugard, who made him read *Zen and the Art of Archery*.

Subsequently, Manim and Simon both resigned from PACT and together formed The Company, mounting plays in hotels and odd theaters for two years until they won a bid to turn the city-controlled Indian Fruit Market into a theater complex with money raised from local industrialists and corporations. Together, they planned to ignore totally the government's segregation laws. Earlier, the supreme court had set a precedent when it allowed producers of *Godspell* to employ a multiracial cast. But while the Space Theatre in Cape Town was open to integrated audiences, not since *King Kong* had blacks and whites in Johannesburg been legally permitted to attend a play together. Government-imposed curfews made it unlawful for blacks to be in the city at night; under South Africa's version of American Jim Crow laws, anyone, black or white, who used the rest room would be guilty of a criminal act. Simon, Manim, and their associates knew that it would take some time to convince black audiences that it was safe for them to go to the theater and to generate the work that would interest them—but that, nonetheless, was their goal.

On June 16, 1976, when the Soweto uprisings ignited, Simon was

presiding over the final week of rehearsals for the Market's first offering, Chekhov's *The Seagull.* If it hadn't been too late to turn back, he
says, he would have canceled the production. Considering that there
was a war raging in the black townships, the cerebral sufferings of
Chekhov's characters seemed inappropriate and unintentionally ironic.
In the first scene, Masha says to the schoolmaster Medvedenko, "I'm
in mourning for my life." And as black children with no property
rights whatever were massacred, literally, at the opposite end of the
Soweto Highway, the white actress playing Masha had to raise a self-
pitying hand to her forehead and say, seriously, before an all-white audience, "You think there's nothing worse than being poor, but if you
ask me, it's a thousand times better to be a beggar and wear rags
than . . . Oh, you can't understand."

The actors were working for a minuscule salary—"for love and
pocket money"[7]—but they still made more than two and a half times
what Ngema was then earning at the aluminum plant in Richard's Bay.

A few months later, the second production, Peter Weiss's *Marat/
Sade* (subtitled "The Persecution and Assassination of Jean-Paul
Marat, as Performed by the Inmates of the Asylum of Charenton
Under the Direction of the Marquis de Sade"), was a more relevant
choice. "The Revolution came and went,/Unrest replaced by discontent." "Napoleon! Nation! Revolution! Copulation!" cried the actors
onstage.

The first show employing a large-scale multiracial cast was *The Me
Nobody Knows,* an American musical about children in New York
City's ghettos. But the first time a production drew a large black audi-
ence was a year after the theater opened, when John Kani and Winston
Ntshona came to perform *Sizwe Banzi Is Dead* and *The Island,* and
sanctioned the Market in the eyes of their devoted black following.

Athol Fugard has said of the Market's genesis that "for the first time
a truly successful attempt was made in one area to put a stop to the waste
of human beings and human potential that had categorized the South African experience up to then."[8] Since it opened in 1976, the Market has
ignored every taboo and law restricting the commingling of races. John
Kani's résumé alone is a testimony to this policy: He has played leads in
such Market productions as *Othello, Miss Julie*—which elicited bomb

threats and hate mail from white conservatives—and *Waiting for Godot.* Kani has directed plays, too, and was ultimately named to the administrative post of associate director.

The Market has given wide, international exposure to the agitprop play, what the South African novelist Nadine Gordimer has called "the first contemporary art form that many black South Africans feel they can call their own."[9] With each year, the emphasis placed on the creation of a new body of South African theater literature has been reinforced. Almost all of the South African plays that have traveled overseas in recent years have come by way of the Market—*Sophiatown, Born in the R.S.A., Bopha, You Strike the Woman You Strike the Rock,* etc. It is the only organization of its kind and scope in South Africa, and consequently it will never succeed in pleasing everybody, hiring every artist who wants a job, or representing every political point of view. But the Market has persevered with a kind of tenacity and stamina that is afforded by few American producing organizations, which are often constrained by the exacting influence of financiers, reviewers, trade unions, and, not infrequently, their own greed.

Director Benjy Francis has worked at the Market over the years, but he's one of the theater's diverse critics. "What the Market is doing comes from the will to do good," he says, "not from any historic organic experience, and the only way it can have that is if it is run by black folk and not just any black folk . . . people with a vision. . . . The danger is that the Market has been alone too long. It's not a rejection of what it is doing, it's the fact that it cannot reach the frustration of the masses."[10]

Robert Kavanagh, the author of the Marxist-leaning *Theatre and Cultural Struggle in South Africa* and editor of *South African People's Plays,* has called the Market *petit bourgeois;* its valuable and sometimes politically hard-hitting work has been diminished in its social effectiveness, in his view, because it's "marketed for the consumption of *petit bourgeois* audiences in South Africa and in various Western countries."[11]

In the early nineties, a decade and a half after the Soweto uprisings, but only barely past the stripping of the Group Areas Act and other apartheid legislation and in the continued absence of universal suffrage, there seemed to be a feeling in some circles that plays presented there had done little more than preach to the converted.

There are remonstrators on the other side, too, who feel that the traditions and tastes of white artists and audiences are underrepresented at the Market; the critic Barry Ronge has been quoted as complaining that "the Market has become a declaration of political intent and that's put reins on what they should be doing dramatically."[12]

There are some commercial and state-run theaters in South Africa, a few annual festivals, some university venues, and PACT, but among people, black and white, who write, direct, and act in plays, the Market has for many years been the locus of their aspirations. Space won't allow listing every play that has been produced there, but it is an amazingly diverse catalogue—classical, contemporary, American, European, and indigenous, in all the languages spoken in South Africa.

With no financial support from the government, it's interesting to note how much of the Market's funding has come from the mining conglomerates and other exploitative businesses that most of the world has shunned throughout the period of the theater's existence. Most South African artists I've met, even the most radical ones, have a far more relaxed attitude about accepting money from such industries than American artists I know who refuse to take support from, for instance, Philip Morris, the cigarette giant, or to wear the running shoes of Reebok, a company that did business in South Africa when sanctions were in place.

The last time I was at the Market, in 1991, Manim, who always held the place together with his extraordinary mettle, his compassionate pragmatism, and his talent for interpersonal bridge-building, had just resigned as managing director to pursue opportunities elsewhere. Still, the Market seemed to have its life force burning. After its sixteen years of existence as the single critical, enduring place of artistic experimentation and activism in South Africa, a country that seems to hunger for theater, the only movement the Market has not been able to foster is its own replication and thus an allowance for more theaters, wider innovation, more voices.

Chapter Eight

▼

Therefore I tell you, whatever you ask in prayer, believe that you have received it, and it will be yours.

The Gospel According to Mark

Simon, Ngema, and Mtwa began their rehearsals for *Our Father Who Art in Heaven,* as their play was then called, on spec, with the agreement that they would be paid by the Market only when they opened to the public. Nonetheless, the actors' fortunes began to improve when they embarked upon this next stage of their work. As their stage manager they recruited Dixon Malele, who had worked for Kente. And Malele introduced them to a generous man known as Bra Vusi.

Bra Vusi possessed considerable means, attained in a Robin Hood–like manner. For some time, a great number of upstanding black South Africans have not necessarily considered encroachments upon the wealth of the white establishment to be criminal or immoral behavior—people who purloin white-owned automobiles, for instance, are often respectfully called "car liberators." Most of the crime in South Africa has been suffered by black people, who until recently have had no binding rights or recourse at all. But for many years, some organized black syndicates have been involved in technically unlawful activities directed exclusively at white-owned property, guided by a moral scripture to which Vusi also attached himself. He was a bank robber by specialty—a highly regarded, bighearted, thick-walled man, who drove a princely Cadillac.

Bra Vusi accepted an invitation to see a run-through of the play, at the end of which he "jumped with joy," according to Malele, and offered to pay a weekly stipend of 35 rand each to Ngema, Mtwa, and Malele. Until then, their daily budget had afforded them only a pint of milk and a half-loaf of brown bread, which they'd shared at lunchtime. But now they could live and eat more decently, and Ngema could contribute a little to Ignatia's household budget. Two weeks later, Vusi's enthusiasm for the play increased, and he doubled the weekly payments.

Rehearsals began somewhat awkwardly. Simon felt that the script should be more closely related to the parables told in the Gospels and proposed some critical revisions. But after the exhilarating audience response to the initial run-through, Ngema and Mtwa were surprised to hear that a major rewrite was considered necessary. They had been alone with the play for so long, and had invested so much of themselves in it, that they had become protective of their work. Although it was Simon's perspicacity that had originally attracted them to him, they felt, at first, a little violated when he applied it to their creation. Simon also asked them to explore Soweto's neighborhoods and Johannesburg's Albert Street—where blacks queued up to apply for work-seekers' permits, and white employers came to find cheap temporary labor—for characters and details of life to enrich the play. This research they stubbornly resisted, for they felt that they already knew all there was to know about Soweto and Albert Street—certainly more than Simon did. It seems that Ngema may have been slightly more willing than Mtwa, who tended to be temperamental and was truly angered by Simon's assumption of authority. But the process was not what either of them had expected. They had never before worked or relaxed with a white person—and Simon was a good two decades older than they. There was a great deal to adjust to.

Simon recalls that Ngema and Mtwa would occasionally consent to do the research in the field, announce that they were on their way, and leave the rehearsal room. Then, later, when they should have been on Albert Street, Simon would find them in the coffee bar in the Market lobby, flirting and socializing. They always had an excuse for being there—usually that Bra Vusi hadn't shown up to transport them in his car. They had walked far greater distances hundreds of times in their lives, but had come to prefer riding in a Cadillac. Unfortunately, the unpredictable nature of Bra Vusi's business made it difficult for him to keep to a schedule.

One day, Simon came down with the flu and sent word to Ngema and Mtwa that they should remain in Soweto to do their research. Simon stayed in bed and invited a friend who was knowledgeable of the New Testament to spend the day instructing him in it. As a Jewish child, Simon had been sent out of the classroom when that part of the Bible was studied in school.

Ngema and Mtwa decided to finally fulfill their assignment and, to their surprise, had a splendid day. They looked at Soweto through new eyes, finding fascination in everyday people they'd overlooked in the past—a barber whose shop consisted of a chair on the side of the road; an old man threading a needle to mend a coat; a young boy selling meat from a cart in the putrefying sun; an old woman scavenging for food in trash heaps. The next day, the three men shared their discoveries. It was a miraculous day, and the play began to coalesce. During subsequent rehearsals, the collaboration flourished.

To avoid offending the censors, who forbade flagrant allusions to Christian icons, they chose to refer to Jesus as "Morena," a Sotho term of deferential address. In the play's final form, the two actors—called "Percy" and "Mbongeni" in the text[1]—metamorphose into scores of characters who, in twenty-six scenes, each one flowing unhesitatingly into the next, react to reports of Morena's appearance in South Africa. The stage is bare, except for a couple of crates and a coatrack holding a few items of ragged clothing and hats that the actors use to aid them in their transformations. When the play begins, they wear nothing but gray track pants and running shoes. And "around each actor's neck is a piece of elastic, tied to which is half a squash ball painted pink—a clown's nose, to be placed over his own nose when he plays a white man."

At the end of the rehearsal process, Ngema, Mtwa, and Simon shared the writing credit equally. Simon's principal authorial contribution seems to have been in guiding the work into a sophisticated structure, refining, poeticizing, and augmenting much of the dialogue, and encouraging the research in Soweto and on Albert Street. But the intensely physical quality of the work stemmed from Ngema's and Mtwa's strenuous independent preparations before they met Simon and their rigorous applications of Grotowski's concepts; in the final script, scenes set on a train vividly conjure their conversations on Kente's bus, which originally fueled the play; and most of the source material traces directly back to their own life experiences.

SCENE ONE:
The actors enter and take their positions quickly, simply. . . . On the first note of their music, overhead lights come on, sculpting them. They become an instrumental jazz band, using only their bodies and their mouths—double bass, saxophone, flute, drums, bongos, trumpet, etc. At the climax of their performance, they transform into audience, applauding wildly.

Percy stands, disappears behind the clothes rail. Mbongeni goes on applauding. Percy reappears wearing his pink nose and a policeman's cap. He is applauding patronisingly. Mbongeni stares at him, stops applauding.

Percy, as the policeman, demands to see Mbongeni's passbook and, examining it, finds that Mbongeni hasn't worked for four years. Mbongeni, true to life, is an itinerant musician. "This is vagrancy," Percy says, "you're unemployed." *To audience:* "*Ja,* this is what I call *loafer-skap!*"

MBONGENI: No, my Colonel, I am a guitarist, I've been playing music for five years, my boss.
PERCY: Hey, you lie, you fuckin' entertainer!
MBONGENI: It's true, it's true, my boss.
PERCY: Can you show me where it is written "musician"? Hey? Where's a guitar? Where's a guitar? Where's a guitar?
MBONGENI: *Ag,nee*—my Brigadier, I am self-employed!
PERCY: Self-employed? *(Chuckling collusively to audience)* Hell, but these kaffirs can lie, hey?
MBONGENI: *Maar, dis die waarheid,* but it is true—my General!

PERCY: You know where you should be?

MBONGENI: No, my boss.

PERCY: You should be in prison!

MBONGENI: No, my boss.

PERCY: And when you come out of prison, do you know where you should go?

MBONGENI: No, my boss.

PERCY: Back to the bush with the baboons. That's where you belong!

Scenes Two, Three, and Four are set in Modder-B Prison, where Mbongeni has been delivered. Conditions in the prison are atrocious, debasing. Percy, his inmate, is a Christian, devoted to Morena; Mbongeni, a religious skeptic, is bitter.

In Scene Five, the two inmates, now free, are reunited some time later on a train, the movement of which is vividly mimed by the actors. "Be careful, my friend," says Percy, "of the anger in your heart. For Morena will return and bear witness to our lives on earth and there will be no place to hide. He will point his holy finger and there will be those who rise to heaven and those who burn in hell. Hallelujah! I hope you're not one of them!"

MBONGENI: Rise to heaven? Where is heaven?

PERCY: It is the Kingdom of God.

MBONGENI: Up there? Neil Armstrong has been there.

PERCY: Neil Armstrong?

MBONGENI: Hallelujah! He's been right up to the moon and he found a desert, no god! . . . And Morena, the saviour, is coming to South Africa?

PERCY: Hallelujah!

MBONGENI: How is he coming to South Africa? By South African Airways jumbo jet?

Mbongeni begins to imagine what would happen if Morena came to South Africa. In Scenes Six, Seven, and Eight, the audience sees how the news would spread through the hysterical media; how the state president would gloat that Morena chose South Africa for the site of his coming. The next several scenes detail the public's reactions. In Scene Nine, an invisible interviewer asks a young Soweto meat vendor—Percy—what he will ask of Morena if he sees him. "I want him to bring me good luck," he says. "So that the people that come will buy all this meat."

SCENE TEN:
Lights up, dim, on Mbongeni as Auntie Dudu, an old woman, wear-ing a white dust-coat as a shawl. She is searching a garbage bin (up-turned box). She eats some food, chases flies, then notices the [invisible] interviewer. She speaks very shyly.
MBONGENI: Hey? My name is Auntie Dudu. No work, my boy, I'm too old. Eh? *(Listens.)* If Morena comes to South Africa? That would be very good. Because everybody will be happy and there will be lots and lots of parties. And we'll find lots of food here *(in-dicates bin)*—cabbages, tomatoes, chicken, hot-dogs, all the nice things white people eat. Huh? *(Receives tip.)* Oh, thank you, my boy. Thank you, Baba.
Inkos'ibusise. God bless you. Bye bye, bye bye. . . .
A fly buzzes close. She chases it.

In Scene Eleven, Percy is the streetside barber. As he cuts Mbongeni's hair, he tells the invisible interviewer that he would like Morena to "build me a barbershop in a very big shopping center in Jo-hannesburg city, with white tiles, mirrors all over the walls, and cus-tomers with big hair!"
In Scene Twelve, the actors play foul-mouthed coal vendors, who think the talk about Morena's coming to South Africa is rubbish.
For Scene Thirteen, Ngema drew from his fascination with Zulu his-tory:

Lights up on Mbongeni entering as a fragile, toothless old man. He sings throughout the following action. He settles on the boxes, at-tempts to thread a needle. His hands tremble but he perseveres. He succeeds on the third laborious attempt and begins to sew a button on his coat.

He becomes aware of the invisible interviewer. Laughs knowingly.

MBONGENI: Eh? What would happen to Morena if he comes to South Africa? What would happen to Morena is what happened to Piet Retief! Do you know Piet Retief? The big leader of the white men long ago, the leader of the Afrikaners! *Ja!* He visited Dingane, the great king of the Zulus! When Piet Retief came to Dingane, Dingane was sitting in his camp with all his men. And he thought, "Hey, these white men with their guns are wizards. They are dangerous!" But he welcomed them with a big smile. He said, "Hello. Just leave your guns outside and come inside and eat meat and drink beer." Eeeeii! That is what will happen to Morena today! The Prime Minister will say, just leave your angels outside and the power of your father outside and come inside and enjoy the fruits of apartheid. And then, what will happen to Morena is what happened to Piet Retief when he got inside. Dingane was sitting with all his men in his camp, when Piet Retief came inside. All the Zulus were singing and dancing . . . *Bamqalokandaba bayimpi . . .* (*Repeats snatches of the song.*) And all the time Dingane's men were singing and dancing, (*proudly*) they were waiting for the signal from their king. And Dingane just stood up. . . . He spit on the ground. He hit his beshu and he shouted *"Bulalan'abathakathi.* Kill the wizards! Kill the wizards! Kill the wizards!" And Dingane's men came with all their spears. (*Mimes throat-slitting, throwing of bodies.*) *Suka!* That is what will happen to Morena here in South Africa. Morena here? (*Disgusted*) Eeii! *Suka!*

In Scenes Fourteen and Fifteen, the actors play airport announcers and newscasters, reporting Morena's arrival at Jan Smuts Airport, Johannesburg.

Scene Sixteen is set on Albert Street. Mbongeni and Percy are now two men competing for the attentions of white employers who drive up looking for workers with valid permits. Then Morena appears to them:

BOTH ACTORS: Morena, look at my pass book!

PERCY: I've got six month special but I can't find work.

MBONGENI: I've been looking here two months, no work. Take us to heaven, Morena, it's terrible here.

Mbongeni follows Morena. Percy falls behind.

PERCY: Temporary or permanent is okay, Morena! *(Silence as Mbongeni converses with Morena. He comes back exhilarated.)* Hey, what does he say?

MBONGENI: He says let us throw away our passes and follow him to Soweto!

PERCY: Hey! He's right! Morena! Morena!

Both actors sing, exhorting the audience:

PERCY: *(under the song)* Morena says throw away your passes and follow him to Soweto.

MBONGENI: We are not pieces of paper, man! We are men!

PERCY: *Ja!* Let them know our faces as Morena knows our faces!

MBONGENI: Morena says no more passes!

PERCY: *Ja!*

MBONGENI: We don't have numbers anymore!

PERCY: *Ja!*

MBONGENI: Let them look at our faces to know that we are men.

PERCY: *Ja!* When we follow Morena we walk as one!

The actors throw away their passes and their song transforms into train sounds.

In Scene Seventeen, we return to the train and the former inmates. While Percy sings, Mbongeni pursues his speculations about Morena's visit to South Africa. He says, "*Ja, madoda,* hundreds of thousands will gather at the Regina Mundi Church in the heart of Soweto . . ."

There will be bread for all. And wine for all. Our people will be left in peace, because there will be too many of us and the whole world will be watching. And people will go home to their beds.

These will be days of joy. Auntie Dudu will find chicken legs in her rubbish bin, and whole cabbages. And *amadoda*—our men— will be offered work at the Pass Office. The barber will be surrounded by white tiles. The young meat-seller will wear a nice new uniform and go to school, and we will all go to Morena for our blessings. *(Song subsides. Percy lies on boxes as sleeping woman.)* And then . . . the government will begin to take courage again. . . . The police and the army will assemble from all parts of the country. . . . And one night, police dogs will move in as they have done before. There will be shouts at night and banging on the door. . . .

Mbongeni's speech is interrupted by a frenzied scene taken directly from Ngema and Mtwa's experiences of midnight police raids at Ignatia's house in Pimville. Percy becomes Ignatia, crying out to her children in Zulu: "They've come to attack us!" Afterward, Mbongeni resumes his speech:

They'll start surrounding our homes at night. And some of our friends will be caught by stray bullets. There will be roadblocks at every entrance to Soweto, and Regina Mundi Church will be full of tear-gas smoke! Then life will go on as before.
He throws his arms up in the air in disgust, cries out.

Scene Eighteen is set in Coronation Brickyard, recalling Ngema's childhood experience as a bricklayer. Morena, still invisible to the audience, appears to two workers. Mbongeni—whom Percy calls "Zuluboy" in this scene—offers him something to eat.

MBONGENI: Are you hungry, Morena? Are you hungry? I've got nice food for you. I've got a packet of chips. *(Mimes.)* It's very good, this one. There's lots of vinegar and salt—I bought them from the shop just around the corner.
PERCY: That's potatoes, Morena.
MBONGENI: I've got half-brown bread. Whole-wheat. You made this long ago, huh? I've been telling Bobbejaan, you made plenty in

the wedding— He's got power, this one! *(Mimes.)* This is Coca-Cola, Morena.

PERCY: It's cold drink.

MBONGENI: For quenching thirst.

PERCY: Ha, Morena, there's no Coca-Cola in heaven?

MBONGENI: What do you drink up there?

They listen, then laugh uproariously. . . .

At the end of the scene, the brickyard is besieged by police pursuing Morena. Zuluboy defends Morena, performing a Zulu war dance, thrusting his knobkerrie at the invisible attackers.

Scene Nineteen: John Vorster Square Prison, Johannesburg. Percy, now a white policeman, describes the previous scene at Coronation Brickyard to his superior, Mbongeni. Although the mad Zuluboy managed to escape, he says, Morena has been detained as a subversive and is presently confined in a tenth-floor interrogation room. Then, out the window, the two men see the angel Gabriel ascending to the tenth floor to free Morena.

In Scene Twenty, we return to the train and the former inmates. Mbongeni imagines what Morena will feel after he has witnessed the abominations of apartheid. Here Ngema makes reference to his former captor, Matanzima.

MBONGENI: Morena will say, I see families torn apart, I see mothers without sons, children without fathers, and wives who have no men! Where are the men? *Aph'amadoda madoda?* And people will say, *Ja,* Morena, it's this bladdy apartheid. It's those puppets, *u* Mangope! *u* Matanzima! *u* Sebe! Together with their white Pretoria masters. They separate us from our wives, from our sons and daughters! And women will say, Morena, there's no work in the homelands. There's no food. They divide us from our husbands and they pack them into hostels like men with no names, men with no lives! And Morena will say, Come to me, you who are divided from your families. Let us go to the cities where your husbands work. We will find houses where you can live together and we will talk to those who you fear! What country is this? *(Spits on the ground.)*

SCENE TWENTY-ONE:
Spotlight finds Percy as Prime Minister, pink nose, spectacles.
PERCY: My people, as your Prime Minister I must warn you that we stand alone in the face of total onslaught. Our enemies will stop at nothing, even to the extent of sending a cheap communist magician to pose as the Morena, and undermine the security of our nation. But let me assure you that this cheap imposter is safely behind bars, from which he cannot fly. Peace and security have returned to our lovely land.

Scene Twenty-two is set in a solitary cell on Robben Island. Mbongeni, a prisoner, talks to Morena through the walls:

Morena, I sit here just like you with this one light bulb and only the Bible to read! . . . So what do you want here? What does your father know? What does he say? Come on, Morena, man! . . . You've got all the power! How can you let these things happen? How can you just sit there like that, Morena? Okay, okay, I know you don't like miracles, but these are bladdy hard times, Morena. Morena, I must tell you, now that I've gone into your book, I really like you, Morena. But I'm getting bladdy disappointed. How long must we wait for you to do something?

Scene Twenty-two flows swiftly into Scene Twenty-three. Mbongeni and Percy are now white guards at the Robben Island prison. "I wish they had kept [Morena] in John Vorster Square or Pretoria Central," Percy says.

MBONGENI: Come on, Corporal. You know what happened at John Vorster Square. Gabriel got him out of there in ten seconds flat! Only Robben Island has got the right kind of AA missiles.
PERCY: AA? What is that?
MBONGENI: Anti-Angel.
PERCY: Anti-Angel? I never heard of that!
MBONGENI: He'll never get away from Robben Island!

PERCY: *(distracted, points into the audience)* Hey! Sergeant! What's that you said? Just look over there! Just look over there!!!

MBONGENI: *(moves lazily toward him, singing "Sarie Marais")* My Sarie Marais is so ver van my hart . . . *(Suddenly he looks into the audience, horrified.)* God! Hey! Fire! Fire!

They riddle the audience with machine-gun fire.

PERCY: Call helicopter control, quick!!!

MBONGENI: Hello? Hello? Radio 1254 CB? Over. Hello? Radio 1254 . . .

In Scene Twenty-four, Mbongeni and Percy, now two helicopter pilots, receive a command to drop bombs on Morena as he escapes from Robben Island by walking on water to Cape Town. In Scene Twenty-five, Percy, as a newscaster, informs South African viewers that the bombing has completely destroyed Cape Town and Table Mountain; he updates the audience on Morena's progress to the mainland.

Scene Twenty-six: An ethereal calm takes hold of the stage. Morena, played by Percy, appears in a graveyard. Mbongeni, as Zuluboy again, guides him in a dance through the cemetery, pointing out the graves of dead heroes of the anti-apartheid struggle. Percy resurrects the heroes, singing a sacred song. He calls *"Woza!"* (Rise up): *"Woza* Albert!" (Albert Luthuli was the first president-general of the ANC). *"Woza* Robert!" (Sobukwe). *"Woza* Steve!" (Biko). . . .

▼

After six weeks of preparation, the play, now called *Woza Albert!,* opened in the sixty-seat Laager Theatre at the Market. The performance was an immediate confrontation of sweat and heat that most audiences had never experienced before in such intensity or in such close quarters—Ngema was a profuse perspirer and always managed to shower the first few rows. The play was an enormous success and drew more blacks to the Market than any previous production. From the Laager, Manim and Simon moved the play onto the main stage and then on an extensive tour of the black townships and homelands—for which Mali Hlatswayo, formerly of Kente's company, painted the promotional banners.

Britain's BBC came to South Africa to cover the national elections taking place that year and filmed some of *Woza Albert!* to illustrate and enliven the story. Later, the director of the piece returned to the country to make an entire documentary film devoted to the play. After the director of the annual theater festival in Edinburgh saw the first program on television, he invited *Woza Albert!* to the Traverse Theatre. And at a performance of the play in an integrated theater in Cape Town, the associate director of Los Angeles's Mark Taper Forum was in the audience. Soon arrangements were being made for trips to Great Britain, Berlin, and America.

Woza Albert! won Edinburgh's Fringe First Award, which Ngema and Mtwa dedicated to Bra Vusi. Later, they won the Los Angeles Drama Critics Award, and soon they were receiving enough invitations from theaters all over the world to keep them on the road for five years, winning almost every award for which they were eligible in the cities they visited. In 1983, they opened at the Lucille Lortel Theatre in New York for an extended run, for which they were awarded an Obie.

It was a tremendously long and arduous tour. Ngema and Mtwa did not always get along well offstage, and sometimes they broke off all personal communication. Mtwa still harbored some resentment for Simon, too, and frequently refused to accept direction from him, using Dixon Malele as an intermediary.

But as unhesitatingly as Ngema had seized upon the notion of becoming a theater artist back in Richard's Bay, he now embraced his new eminence. When they opened in the Laager, Ngema and Mtwa went on the Market Theatre payroll and rented an inexpensive house in Pimville. When the house burned to the ground—they inadvertently left a candle burning when they went to the theater one night—Ngema had nowhere to go but to the Market, where he slept in the bar-lounge on a leatherette banquette; he was locked inside each night at closing time and had to take great care not to set off the alarm system. But by the time the show opened in San Francisco, only a few months later, Ngema had acquired a rich man's fastidiousness. Barney Simon says: "My hotel room to me was a miracle. Mbongeni's room was very similar—identical, really, maybe a slightly better view. But he didn't like it and insisted on moving to another. And I couldn't understand why. It happened very quickly, his move into this other mode."

Ngema instantly adapted to his new status with the ease and confidence of someone who had been born with money and prestige. His wealth was relative—when Khassi had a steady job and a few taxis, he was considered affluent; Ngema was now only slightly better off than he was—but his accomplishments immediately elevated him to a position of social prominence.

Seven years after *Woza* opened, the commercial success of *Sarafina!*, which moved from the Market to Lincoln Center Theater in New York and then quickly onto Broadway, and spawned a second company to tour Europe and Japan, gave him the means to buy whatever tempted him—musical instruments, cars, recording equipment, clothes in bulk quantities—not just in South Africa, where the dollars he earned abroad were disproportionately commanding, but in New York, the most expensive city in America. If no producer was willing to pay for a first-class ticket from South Africa to New York, where *Sarafina!* was playing, he would buy the upgrade himself. And he was just as unselfconscious stretched out amid the white lawyers and moguls sharing the cabin as he had been sleeping on the banquette in the bar at the Market.

Barney Simon recalls that when *Woza Albert!* was in London, he said to Ngema, " 'Just understand that a lot of things are going to happen to you and I'm on your side.' And that was a commitment to something I recognized as being extraordinary." Simon compares Ngema to a great athlete—like a young John McEnroe, who had not only the physical gifts but also the confidence necessary to succeed and the ability to hold all the dimensions of the court and the game in his mind at the same time. "To me there's something about Mbongeni that is almost like an act of nature," Simon says. "There's a way in which he persists in what he wants to do. He works out of a vision. You can cut down Mbongeni—and there is a lot of criticism of him here. You can say, 'Ah, well, this is just Gibson Kente with money,' but Mbongeni is a phenomenon in his own right. Whether he's eclectic or not is not the issue. When we were creating *Woza,* the Zulus he created came from a powerful perception of what people are, and it's a loving perception. It's powerful, and a great gift. On that level I think he's unassailable. He's able to achieve what he achieves through having a sense of how things can be."

CHAPTER NINE

▼

[W]hen an actor moves before us at last with the strange freedom and calm of one possessed by the real, we are stirred as only the theater can stir us.

ROBERT EDMOND JONES[1]

In a Greenwich Village town house in January 1988, just a few days before *Sarafina!* moved from Lincoln Center's 300-seat Mitzi Newhouse Theatre to the 1,100-seat Cort Theatre on Broadway, Ngema met with Peter Brook, whose manifesto *The Empty Space* had encouraged and validated him for many years, to discuss the parallels in their work. Brook was a few days away from an opening too, of his production of *The Cherry Orchard* at the Majestic Theatre in Brooklyn.

It wasn't their first meeting. Almost two years earlier, Brook, who has lived in Paris since the early 1970s, when he founded the International Center of Theatre Research at the Bouffes du Nord, was in New York to cast a multicultural, English-language production of his epic work *The Mahabharata.* One of his colleagues heard that a new play from South Africa, *Asinamali!,* had just arrived in Harlem, at the Roger Furman Theatre. Brook rushed to the Furman and caught the first half of the play, which enthralled him. "I don't really enjoy going to the theater as such," Brook later said, "unless there is that particular current between a play and an audience that turns it into something alive. We weren't even prepared to go there. We had something else on that evening and had to leave before the end, leaving word that, more than anything, I wanted to meet Mbongeni."[2]

Ngema wrote and directed *Asinamali!* but did not perform in it. Brook had never seen Ngema's work as an actor, but when they met a few days later, he offered Ngema the crucial role of Krishna in *The Mahabharata*. "The only way of playing it," he later told Ngema, "would be to irradiate Krishna with everything you have developed and acquired in your self in your life."

The structural basis for *Asinamali!* was a real-life rent strike, spearheaded by a heroic man named Msizi Dube in 1983 in the black township of Lamontville, outside Durban. When Dube was gunned down by government forces, his death inflamed his followers. Through a kaleidoscopic presentation of song, story, and pantomime, the five actors of *Asinamali!* delineate the passages of five unrelated men—each with at least some tangential connection to the martyred Dube—to one common prison cell. One man is a swindler and a thief; one was arrested under the Immorality Act for having sexual relations with a white woman; one for murdering his girlfriend; one for his activities as a hard-line devotee of Msizi Dube; another for being an unwitting accessory in the murder of one of the black policemen who killed Dube.

Brook, asked what most impressed him about *Asinamali!,* said:

First of all, the tremendous quality of the group work. It reached a point at which the group was behaving like one person with five heads. There was a perfect interrelation at tremendous speed. If one hand went out to the right, it was caught by a foot which was going to the left or a mouth making a sound.

The second thing was the basis of the work. If one had to say what is the first reality in the theater, some people would say it's the ideas. Others would say the subject matter. I think the first reality, what every subject matter sits on, is a flow of energy. . . .

With that as the basis, then what I found most interesting is in relation to the meaning of the play and the South African context. If you approach a situation like the South African one naturalistically, you can't present terrible events like these in any other than a tragic, sentimental way. The events in their very nature are tragic or sentimentality-producing events. But what I found profoundly right and extraordinary about *Asinamali!* was that this horrifying situation was being presented, pitilessly, through a *joie de vivre*. The events were not softened by it, but heightened to the last degree because they were presented, not through a sentimentality, but through a vitality.

In fact, Ngema did develop *Asinamali!* from a core of group energy and not from any particular thematic concept or plot—the events in Lamontville actually occurred *after* he started rehearsals. The inspiration to begin the work on the play came to him when he was in Los Angeles with *Woza Albert!* There he met Luis Valdez, who founded his company, El Teatro Campesino, in 1966 with Chicanos recruited from the National Farm Workers Association. Valdez's earliest work was bilingual propaganda theater performed on the back of a flatbed truck for striking grape pickers in Delano, California. Later, he incorporated his knowledge of commedia dell'arte, Brecht, and Mayan mysticism to expand the work, to create a theater that would, in his words, "universalize the Chicano movement." Motivated by Valdez's example to surround himself with accomplished artists dedicated not only to the work of the theater but to the advancement of their people, Ngema returned to South Africa and founded his own company, which he called Committed Artists. He rented an unfurnished house in Umlazi township and installed a group of young men there, including Bheki Mqadi, from the *Too Harsh* company, and Ngema's younger brother Bhoyi. For three years, between legs of the *Woza* tour, he returned to instruct them in Kente's vocal drills and Grotowski's physical exercises, and to uncover, through group improvisation, the ideas and structure for a new play. When the rent strike broke out in Lamontville, resulting in Dube's martyrdom, he found the linchpin for the work. In 1985, *Asinamali!* (Dube's rallying cry, meaning: "We have no money!") played in a cinema in Soweto before opening to great acclaim at the Market Theatre; then followed a national and an international tour, culminating in a brief Broadway engagement. The play won numerous awards around the world and a Tony nomination for Ngema's work as a director.

In the tradition of African storytelling, the play begins in the simplest, most direct manner possible:[3]

The stage is bare, save for five prison chairs at the center, and to the lefthand corner a coatrack that is suspended from the roof. It serves two purposes, as a coatrack, then a window. There are two coats and a hard hat.

Five actors walk to the stage in semidarkness. Four of them are in khaki prison attire and one is in his regular clothes (Bheki). They sit on the chairs.

SONG: "Fanakalo" [All songs are a cappella.]

BHEKI *(jumps up mid-song and moves downstage, on top of the music):* I come from Zululand. I got a place to stay in Lamontville township, near the white city of Durban. During that time this man *(he points to his T-shirt, which has the picture of a man)* Msizi Dube, a very strong leader and a powerful voice for our people, was killed. They killed him. The government spies killed him. The reason for his death was that he maintained that we have no money. A-SI-NA-MA-LI! So we cannot afford to pay the government's high rent increase. People took up this call: "AAASSSIIINNNAAA MMMAAALLLIII!" and the police went to work. Many of us died and many of us went to jail, and it is still happening outside.

SONG: "Heshe Nsizwa"

BONGANI: *(moves downstage, stuttering):* I come from Zululand too. I left my four wives and twelve children back in Zululand. My cousins got me work in . . . in . . . in . . .

ALL *(in rhythm with the song):* Johannesburg.

BONGANI: Yeah! At a road construction. After many people had been fired for asking for more money. My white boss thought I was no good. A trouble maker. A follower of Msizi Dube. I lost my job, but I remained in . . . in . . . in . . .

ALL: Johannesburg.

BONGANI: Yeah! I got a girlfriend, a bitch. She fell pregnant. But there was no money to support the child. So she strangled the child in the toilet. I killed her too. And that's why I . . . I . . . I . . . *(motions with his hand to indicate that he wants to say I am here in prison).*

SOLOMZI *(moves downstage, still on top of same song):* I also knew about this man, Msizi Dube. But was not impressed. I come from Soweto. I never really got involved with politics, I got involved with Brother Anthony *(says it with admiration),* we called him "Bra Tony." Heh, heh, heh *(laughs).* Bra Tony, he was a good man. Brilliant pickpocketer. Very intelligent. He knew exactly where the money was in a man's body. He understood a man's body very well. Haaa Bra Tony, he was like Dr. Chris Barnard.

THAMI *(moves downstage):* I come from the Afrikaner farm in Bloemfontein, Orange Free State. Me and my white boss's wife, Mrs. Van Niekerk . . . heh, heh *(indicates that they were making love).* Ya, and she liked it.

BHOYI *(moves downstage):* I come from Lamontville Township, Durban. The follower of Msizi Dube. I was one of the people who were cleaning the streets of the township. The streets of the township were dirty, full of informers. Government spies. But we did it, man. We cleaned them up *(indicates by running his hand across his throat to show a cut-throat motion).*

SONG: "Heshe Nsizwa"
They do a Zulu dance and then rearrange the five chairs to prepare for the court scene. Fade.

▼

With the foundation for the five disparate stories set, the play takes off in all directions, weaving, splintering, and, finally, merging. With no intermission, *Asinamali!*'s thirteen scenes flow seamlessly and robustly. In the authoritative role of sole author and director—or maestro—Ngema meticulously scored the rhythms and tempos as if each scene were a movement in a ninety-minute musical composition, building to a crescendo. The performances were driven by the same athleticism that Ngema and Mtwa applied to *Woza Albert!*

Asinamali!'s first overseas engagement was for three weeks in the spring of 1986 at the minimally equipped Furman Theatre, where

Brook saw the play. Many who attended the earliest performances
have said that the experience was the finest they'd ever had in the theater. The current of energy uniting the actors with the audience, which
Brook admired, was intensified and vitalized in those shows by the exhilaration of five young men on their first trip out of South Africa, in
their first, empathetic meeting with African-Americans. But the performances were also keenly underscored by the fresh memory of a real-
life tragedy that befell the company immediately before it left for New
York: In the course of an extensive last-minute tour of one-nighters,
Asinamali! wended its way from the Johannesburg ghettos, through
the townships of rural Natal, and to a town called Hammarsdale,
where a man was murdered.

This was two years into a fierce wave of nationwide unrest, during
which the South African government reportedly spent, furtively, more
than $1 million to train followers of Gatsha Buthelezi's political move-
ment, Inkatha, as paramilitary hit squads, which were then used to in-
cite violence in Natal's black communities. Because *Asinamali!*
glorified Dube, an adherent of the ANC, which Inkatha vehemently
opposed, the play was incendiary in rural Natal, Buthelezi's strong-
hold. Ngema received a number of personal threats, which he tried to
disregard, from Inkatha disciples pressuring him to cancel the tour.
The people residing in the communities on *Asinamali!*'s Natal itinerary
lived in constant fear of Inkatha-ANC violence, and many stayed away
from the play. Consequently, despite the rave reviews in Johannesburg,
this leg of the tour was not a financial success. And throughout the
week preceding March 22, when the company was scheduled to perform in Hammarsdale, the problem was compounded by a heavy rain
that kept even the bravest theater aficionados at home.

Ngema suggested to his tour manager, Jeff, that they cancel the re-
mainder of the schedule and relax a little before traveling to New York
a week later. Ngema and Jeff were the same age, very close friends, and
they rarely disagreed—they even resembled each other physically and
dressed alike in expensive American styles and jaunty leather caps. But
in this instance Jeff differed with Ngema and argued strongly that to
cancel at this point would be a rash and senseless move. To promote
the Hammarsdale performance, he told Ngema, Mali Hlatswayo had

distributed more than the usual number of publicity banners around the township and generated a great deal of community interest in the show. Furthermore, Jeff said, he had already arranged for special security. He persuaded Ngema that the weather would improve, Inkatha would behave, and the performance would be a success. The five actors, rattled by the threats that had stalked them for weeks, begged Ngema to cancel. But Ngema trusted his manager's judgment—Jeff knew the region well—and the show went on.

At about 5:30 P.M. on March 22, Ngema went to Hammarsdale. The company *kombi* was parked outside the community hall; the man Jeff had hired as a security guard and chauffeur was in the driver's seat. The actors had retired to a house nearby to rest before the performance. Mali Hlatswayo was busy adjusting banners. Makalo Mofokeng, the stage manager, had finished setting the stage lights they carried with them everywhere and was now arranging folding chairs, also property of the *Asinamali!* company, in rows for the audience. Outside, local people were milling around. A man approached Ngema to tell him how much he had liked *Woza Albert!* As he listened, Ngema noticed vaguely that some men across the street were squinting at him studiously. "Is that him?" he heard one say. Ngema called Hlatswayo over and told him that he was going home to Umlazi to fetch his wife, Xoliswa, and that he'd return in time to see the show. And then he slipped away.

Because there was no dressing room or backstage area in the performance hall, the actors dressed in the *kombi* and made their entrance through the main door at the back of the auditorium, singing their way up the center aisle. As they mounted the stage they thought they heard gunshots fired outside, but the audience didn't seem to notice. Hoping they were mistaken, the actors proceeded with the performance.

The audience was divided into two parts—Inkatha partisans on one side of the aisle, stone-faced through even the moments of outrageous humor; on the other side, ANC supporters and sympathetic independent thinkers who enjoyed the play, laughing and crying aloud. From the stage, Ngema's brother Bhoyi heard occasional whispers from the Inkatha side: "Is that him?" someone said. "No, no, he's too young," was the hushed response.

Midway through the performance, Mofokeng and Jeff noticed that a group of men, enveloped in an unmistakable aura of malevolence, had arrived outside. Then police cars and ambulances, all connected to Inkatha and controlled by Buthelezi's KwaZulu administration, pulled up in front of the hall . . . and waited. At every access leading in and out of town, the KwaZulu police were setting up roadblocks.

At the end of the show, the actors exited as they had entered, singing up the aisle and out the main door. But instead of turning them around and sending them back in to take a bow, as had been planned, Mofokeng ushered them directly into the *kombi,* blocking them from the view of the men across the street. Then the guard delivered them to the house where they'd rested earlier.

When they saw that the actors were not going to return for a curtain call, both sides of the audience seemed to assume that the show wasn't over—that this break was an intermission—and calmly emptied out of the hall to stretch their legs and smoke before the start of the second act. Then Mofokeng and Jeff jumped inside and bolted the doors— their immediate concern was to protect the equipment. They listened through the door to the calm chattering and mumbling of the audience on the other side. Then the quality of the noise began to change. Men outside were shouting now, violently, and pounding on the doors; some began to throw stones against the building. Mofokeng and Jeff shouted back, trying to reason with them. But when a petrol bomb was thrown in through a window, they abandoned negotiations, and the stage equipment, and dived for the fire escape. As he climbed down from the window, Mofokeng heard someone say through the dark, "Here they come!" Jeff ran in one direction, and Mofokeng ran in the other, toward the back of the hall.

Adrenaline coursed through Mofokeng as he ran. Well over six feet tall, he hurled himself without hesitation over a fence equal to him in height, and landed directly in the middle of a clutch of Inkatha men lying in wait. Taken off guard, the men shrieked; Mofokeng screamed, too, and kept running toward the bush. Born and raised in Johannesburg, Mofokeng was not even remotely familiar with this area. As he ran a random course in the black night, from street to street, across yards and driveways, the neighborhood dogs yapped and howled at him. He heard the footfalls and voices of men pursuing him—"He's over there"; "I see him over here." Finally, he lost his stalkers and found himself at the gate to a black technical college. He tried to suppress his heavy breathing, to act as if nothing were wrong, when he told the guard at the gate that he was looking for some friends who were students there. But the guard wouldn't let him in. And Mofokeng took off again at high speed, hurdling fences, stumbling through strange neighborhoods. Then he recognized a house he'd seen the night before—it belonged to a member of the *mbaqanga* band The Soul Brothers, who were Ngema's good friends. No one was home. But parked out front was the inhabitant's jeep, blanketed with a canvas sheet. Mofokeng crawled inside and waited; then he realized that he wasn't completely obscured from sight, so he climbed out and stood in the shadows until the man who lived there came home and drove him back to the hall to see what had happened to the others, to the equipment, and to the *kombi*.

The performance hall was desolate now except for three policemen. Mofokeng discovered that the stage lights had been destroyed, the police had taken the folding chairs for safekeeping, and the *kombi* had been damaged. Then he went to the police station, where he found Mali Hlatswayo.

Shortly after the company had arrived at their safe haven, they were discovered by men armed with shotguns. The actors, still in costume, dispersed and fled into the bush. Bheki Mqadi and Bhoyi Ngema made their way to the police station, where they found Hlatswayo, who sent them in a car to Ngema's house in Umlazi.

Much earlier that evening, when Ngema arrived at home, he found his wife dressed and ready to go to the theater. But seeing that there was time to spare, he asked Xoliswa to draw him a bath. Afterward, he asked her to give him a quick message and promptly fell asleep. Hours later, at two in the morning, he woke to a pounding on his door; Mqadi and Bhoyi were breathing heavily as they related their chaotic story. Soon the other actors arrived. At four in the morning, Mofokeng and Hlatswayo showed up, each with his own account. The only one they hadn't heard from was Jeff. But because Jeff was the one among them who was most familiar with the area, they felt sure that he'd hidden himself away somewhere safe.

Then, a few hours later the security guard surfaced and reported that Jeff had been found: hacked to death with bush knives, axes, and spears, and decapitated by men who mistook him for Ngema.

Ngema canceled the rest of the tour. Devastated by the monstrous murder, he and the *Asinamali!* company fled to Johannesburg, where they would be safe. They didn't dare return to Natal for Jeff's funeral—when the killers discovered their mistake, there was a good chance they'd hunt down Ngema.

A week after the Hammarsdale incident, the Committed Artists were on a plane to New York, where, still possessed by the real horror and outrage of Jeff's murder, they were immediately confronted with an audience. In Scene Thirteen, Bhoyi's character describes the killing of his dear friend Bhekani. Though the details of the account differed from the experience Bhoyi had just come from, he saw Jeff clearly when he spoke:

One day soldiers and police came to our school. Bhekani picked up a stone and hit one soldier who was on top of a tank. That was the beginning of shit. We scattered. I threw myself under the barbed-wire fence and I saw Bhekani's feet passing over my head running down the vegetable garden, a policeman right behind him. Ay, that policeman was running like Zola Budd man.
They all laugh.
He caught Bhekani by his shirt. Bhekani came out of the shirt and this policeman had Bhekani's shirt in his hands. His police hat was flying up, his boots were heavy and he was running. We were laughing.
They all laugh and scream.
Bhekani was laughing too. Just around the corner, I saw one policeman pick up a machine-gun. Tratatatatatatata. *(Pointing it towards Solomzi, who then falls in response)* And then I saw Bhekani taking long strides, lifting up into the air, over the vegetable gar-

den fence and then a somersault. And then he hit the ground. That man, my friend, he lay there and he was no longer the man I knew.

▼

Less than two months after *Asinamali!* arrived in New York, the South African government decreed a nationwide state of emergency, giving the police and the military unchecked license to use draconian means in their work and severely restricting all media. But the *Asinamali!* company was at the very beginning of a long international tour, which would take them throughout America, Europe, Japan, and Australia, and keep them far away from the turmoil at home for more than two years.

CHAPTER TEN

▼

People must talk now and tell their story
They must move without fear
Nor should they raise their voices to the hurricanes
But must with their power command them to silence.

MAZISI KUNENE[1]

Ngema chose not to play Krishna in Peter Brook's *Mahabharata,* because it would have taken him away from his own work. As soon as he sent *Asinamali!* on tour, he was already developing the idea for his next play: *Sarafina!* a full-blown musical with a large company of teenagers, a celebration of South Africa's youth, who since 1976 had been at the forefront of the struggle against apartheid.

When he wasn't traveling with the *Asinamali!* company, Ngema was in the Durban townships, looking for potential talent. From church choirs, dance associations, political rallies, ordinary parties, the streets, and his own extended family, he recruited twenty teenagers. Then he moved them into a four-room house in Daveyton, near Johannesburg, lived with them, and trained them vocally, mentally, and physically. And in the course of eight months he developed gradually, as he had in the case of *Asinamali!,* the structure and text of the play, simultaneously composing songs and writing lyrics. For the popular band The Soul Brothers he had written a hit single, "Stimela Sase-Zola," which he sang on their record and which bolstered his confidence as a composer. Jazz trumpeter Hugh Masekela, from his place of exile, agreed to contribute some songs to the show. Ngema hired former Kente star Ndaba Mhlongo, Mary Twala's husband, as choreographer and as conductor of the onstage band, and, to be company manager, Mali Hlatswayo, who had to give up his beloved banner-writing career indefinitely.

Ngema ran rehearsals in the backyard straight through the nights. The twenty teenagers became a family. Intracompany romance was taboo. They ate together and began and ended their workday with group prayer. Every actor, whether included in the scene under examination or not, was required to attend every rehearsal. The players became as unselfconscious in the company of one another as they were among their real brothers and sisters and, consequently, fearless in their acting. They commented on each other's work and shared personal stories relating to the events in the play. Some of these accounts were incorporated into the final script. But the main purpose of the exchanges was to instill in the actors a sense that what was happening to them onstage was as real as anything that had happened to them in life.

They learned the terminology of the theater and inscribed the words in tightly held notebooks—"upstage," "downstage," "apron," "full front," "entrance," "exit," "postmortem." . . . They learned about Peter Brook and Jerzy Grotowski and how to approach a role—through "imagination, visualization, observation, and simulation." Ngema planned a funeral scene and took the company to a cemetery, where they observed and duplicated the technique of gravediggers. They were taught the distinctions between terms Mbongeni had incorporated into his own developing lexicon: projection, diction, levels, intonation. They learned that in Ngema's dramatic theory there are five types of actor: the Method Actor, the Technical Actor, the Stereotyped Actor, the Mechanical Actor, and the Balanced Actor. In their notebooks they wrote:

Balanced Actor
Is the perfectional actor. Combination of
techniques and emotions result in a miracle.
He is versatile, takes control of emotion.

Discipline
Discipline of the mind
Discipline of the body
Discipline of the voice.

What Is Drama
It is human conflict put on stage before an
audience in action and dialogue.

Qualities of Being an Actor
Must have love for theater
Must have dedication
Must have devotion.

Grotowski's Holy Actor
A "holy" actor is that actor whose love, devotion,
and dedication to theater supersedes all
other world and material discipline.

Acting is the basis of life; *Theater* is a
place of investigating the true nature of
life; to *Captivate* is to bring over, to be
magnificent; the *Spontaneous* is something you
do without planning, that comes in a moment.

The *Sarafina!* company dedicated themselves eagerly to the theater
over all other worldly and material considerations, and to Ngema. Almost without exception, these were young people who had never seriously considered a career in the arts—until they met Ngema, there had
been no possibility of such a future. Before they were extricated from
their customary lives, some dared to dream of becoming truckdrivers,
of graduating from high school and going on to trade school, of learning to be secretaries. Some were involved in illicit activities, such as organized shoplifting rings, or were busy attending political rallies and
staging boycotts. A number of them were already parents, though
none were married. Then Ngema chose them and offered an

undreamed-of opportunity. They were willing to make every effort for him. And he took total command of their lives.

Sarafina, the title character (played by Leleti Khumalo), is a beautiful girl with a fierce revolutionary spirit. A leader of students at Morris Isaacson High School in Soweto, she is pursued romantically by all the boys and is the pet of her dauntless and charismatic teacher, Mistress It's a Pity (originally played with gusto by fifteen-year-old Baby Cele). At the outset, Mistress proposes that the students write a class play to perform for the year-end school concert. Sarafina suggests a play about Nelson Mandela (who was still four years away from freedom in 1986, when *Sarafina!* rehearsals began) and is unanimously chosen to play the lead role. The school concert is forgotten, however, until the very end of the evening.

Sarafina! is kaleidoscopic, like *Woza Albert!* and *Asinamali!* The audience is presented with vivid, expressionistic tableaux, breathtaking dancing, and clear, unfaltering voices singing rich harmonies. In the course of events, Sarafina is detained by the police and later released. She tells the story of her mentor, the martyred lawyer Victoria Mxenge. Other characters tell stories, to each other and the audience, about themselves and people they know who have suffered under apartheid; about the high school itself, which in 1976 was "a parliament for black students" involved in the Soweto uprisings. When a soldier overhears Mistress teaching the students about Libya, he absurdly accuses her of being a communist and beats her. Then the school is besieged by the army—represented onstage by one actor—which massacres a large number of the student body. Children are dying in the aisles, wailing onstage; when the soldier turns his machine-gun fire on them, they convulse graphically. Smoke fills the air. Then follows a soulful funeral for the victims of the bloodbath. The actors play the characters they have established for themselves in the first scene, and then, suddenly, they assume the guise of other, symbolic figures. Laws of time and chronology are not strictly adhered to. And at the end comes a relentless outburst of optimism and hope when the school concert is presented in full. Until this moment, we have seen the actors dressed only in their black school uniforms; now they explode onto the stage in traditional skins and brightly colored fabrics. The last entry in the concert is the class play: Sarafina appears, beaming, in men's clothing—as a freed Mandela, she delivers a speech to the nation on "the day of liberation" and invokes the memory of many of the martyred heroes of the struggle.

Although thematically Sarafina is the central figure in the play, the actress playing her is not the "star" in the conventional sense. We come to know half a dozen characters by name during scenes of dialogue and soliloquy. But for each of the twenty musical numbers in *Sarafina!* a new, unidentified member of the chorus, whose voice most genuinely expresses the feeling of the composition, steps forward to take the lead vocal, while the characters we've come to think of as protagonists recede into the chorus. In an American musical like *Fiddler on the Roof,* each musical number advances the story or defines some aspect of the character singing the lead vocal. But the structure that supports *Sarafina!* is based on rules of musical composition, orchestration, and harmony, and not on Aristotle's *Poetics* or any concept of the "well-made play." Each song is an abstract, spiritual expression, arising organically, as songs do in South African life, out of group experience and feeling. The audience becomes intimately involved with the characters moving about before them, living onstage for nearly three hours, displaying every shade of pathos and humor.

Nadine Gordimer has written that "the difficulty, even boredom, many whites experience when reading stories or watching plays by blacks in which, as they say, 'nothing happens,' is due to the fact that the experience conveyed is not 'the development of actions' but 'the representation of conditions,' a mode of artistic revelation and experience for those in whose life dramatic content is in its conditions."[2] Although even its harshest critics would not call *Sarafina!* boring, it, like *Woza Albert!* and *Asinamali!* and the stories Gordimer refers to, has no real plot.

After a successful engagement at the Market Theatre, the company flew to New York. Riding through Manhattan on a bus from the airport, they were amazed at how many white people there were on the streets, for in Johannesburg, blacks are the overwhelming majority. The next day, they were taken on an exhilarating tour of Harlem. The day after that, they met in a rehearsal room at Lincoln Center. Throughout the week approaching opening night, Ngema rewrote the play and improved the choreography. An hour before the first curtain, he was teaching the company a new song to go into the show at a later date. At the time, no one in the cast had any idea how long they'd stay in New York. They were at the mercy of the box office. The original Lincoln Center engagement was extended repeatedly, and then the production moved to Broadway, where it played to full houses for a year and a half.

Upon arriving in New York, the company stayed at the swanky Mayflower Hotel on Central Park West. They kept late hours and played loud music; every time someone in the company had a birthday, there was a raucous party. Finally asked to leave by the management, they relocated to the Esplanade Hotel on West End Avenue, where they occupied efficiency apartments with kitchenettes. With each extension of their stay, however, their infatuation with New York waned and they grew more deeply homesick. They discovered that America is a racist country too: taxi drivers wouldn't stop for them no matter how nicely they were dressed; a group of the *Sarafina!* men were rudely grilled by inhospitable police in Times Square for an hour one night because they weren't carrying their passports. In their melancholy, many of the actors called South Africa several times a day and accrued telephone bills in the thousands of dollars. They cooked South African food that reminded them of their mothers. The then exiled singer and icon Miriam Makeba, whom they'd never met, came to a performance; afterward, she led them in a Zulu song that stirred such deep feelings of longing in some of the girls that they sobbed uncontrollably. During the course of the two years that they performed in New York, a few of the actors lost parents at home and were unable to return for the funerals. Heads hung low backstage in empathic grief; provisional memorial services were held in hotel rooms.

But they also made money. Many, in the delirium of sudden solvency, squandered their income on the goods displayed enticingly in Times Square along the route to the theater—stereos, electronic keyboards, VCRs, leather goods. Others managed to send formidable sums home, which their families used to build houses, send children to school, erect deluxe marble tombstones in honor of the deceased, and buy food and clothes.

The actors had a number of opportunities to educate themselves during their stay in America. A few took high school courses and then equivalency exams. Some learned to play musical instruments. Others let the opportunity pass.

They were honored and celebrated. They performed in the nationally televised Tony Awards ceremony. The show received five nomination: best musical, featured actress—Khumalo—score, choreography, and direction. They met so many major stars, who came to see the show, that they became blasé at the sight of a famous face. Still, every night before the performance they gathered for group prayer. When Ngema was in town, he convened the company in his hotel room sometimes straight through the night, to critique their work, to hear grievances, to teach new songs he intended to put into the show. He recorded a solo album, *Time to Unite,* for which they sang backup vocals. They also made a sound-track recording of *Sarafina!,* which received a Grammy nomination, and sang on records by Ziggy Marley, Michael Bolton, and Third World. Academy Award–winning director Nigel Noble made a feature-length documentary film about them; his camera crew followed them everywhere for months.

Ngema was constantly flying in and out of South Africa and was frequently asked by the foreign press to explain why he and his actors had been granted passports to perform overseas what was clearly a subversive work. Knowing only that the South African government was guided by unfathomable and duplicitous motives, he repeatedly replied: "They handed me a passport, I was glad to have it, and I didn't ask why." Nadine Gordimer has written that when she was interviewed abroad, she often detected this implied skepticism in questions from reporters: "If my country really was a place where such things happened, how was it I could write about them?" The *Sarafina!* actors heard the same doubting tones in America.

Perhaps the South African officials who in 1987 decided to give passports to Ngema and to the twenty-three actors in *Sarafina!* who shouted "We know the government is shit!" onstage every night knew about this wariness in foreigners. Perhaps it seemed to them that there was a good chance that an American audience wouldn't see the documentary reality in *Sarafina!*—that it would be seen as another feel-bad/feel-good musical melodrama like *Les Misérables.* It may have seemed more sensible to take that risk than to let a more respected and farther-reaching medium, like the TV news, announce that South Africa was denying Mbongeni Ngema his freedom of speech and his freedom of travel.

Ngema traveled constantly. He, assembled a second company, rehearsed them in Johannesburg, and sent them on a tour of Europe and Japan. In 1989, this company went to Paris and performed at Peter Brook's Bouffes du Nord as part of the nationwide celebration of the bicentennial of the French Revolution. Following *Sarafina!,* Brook mounted a French-language production of *Woza Albert!,* which he directed himself with two West African actors.

A little earlier, Brook had organized a tribute at his theater for his friend Jerzy Grotowski, who had been conducting paratheatrical laboratories in Italy for some years, in a kind of self-imposed exile from the public stage. Ngema flew to Paris for the event. Before the public affair, he met with Grotowski alone in Brook's office and found that, in spite of the arcane gravity of his work, the man himself was hearteningly simpatico—a kindred spirit. They shared the same earthy sense of humor. Ngema told Grotowski about a dramatic principle he was cultivating, which he calls "theater of the ancestors": A character in a play tells a story about his deceased father. The actor may not have written the speech himself, but he has filtered his performance through the remembrance of an analogous personal experience, the memory of his own father. As he tells the story, three lives breathe at once through the actor: his own, his character's, and his ancestor's. This, Ngema says, Grotowski easily understood. They spoke freely, like old friends.

Chapter Eleven

▼

Again I felt rich, increased, to be loved by two women. Yes, that was it: to be loved by two women. More than that, I loved them both; each in a different way.

Es'kia Mphahlele,
Chirundu[1]

In 1981, Ngema's family received the first news of their absent son since 1978, when they'd seen his name in an advertisement for *Too Harsh*. Now, they read, he was performing again, this time in eGoli (the City of Gold, as the Zulus call Johannesburg), in a play called *Woza Albert!,* which he'd written in collaboration with a white man—this they found to be most mysterious and tantalizing information.

A few months later, Ngema suddenly reentered the life of his family. A strange Mazda hatchback turned off the main byway and into the Ngema homestead in Hlabisa. The children playing in the road stopped their games to watch a young man in stylish city clothes step out of the car, which was stuffed with groceries and gifts. Seven years after Ngema had left his grandfather's farm to become a migrant laborer, he returned a showbiz star.

He began to send money regularly for school fees, food, other family exigencies, and the first pair of shoes his sixteen-year-old brother, Nhlanhla, had ever owned. When *Woza* toured to Durban, Ma Hadebe went to see the play. Afterward, Ngema, feeling flush, took her to Wimpy's for hamburgers with all the trimmings, pampering her in a way she was completely unaccustomed to. But in the seven years since the family had last seen him, he had acquired more than just relative material wealth. Ngema had become a grown man, with a new and urbanized life that they could hardly fathom. And he had gained a wife, who was not a Zulu but a Xhosa.

Ngema met Xoliswa Nduneni in 1979 in the Transkei when he was on tour there with Kente's company. A student at an Umtata boarding school, she was the younger sister of a girlfriend of Percy Mtwa's. She met Ngema at a cast party after his performance and held him in awe as a wonderful actor, but she was only sixteen years old and found the drinking, smoking, and debauchery in the Kente company to be a little terrifying. She saw that Ngema was surrounded by adoring local women, and she didn't even consider the possibility of romance. But she was a tall, slender, and intelligent girl, who carried herself with grace and dignity and had a beautiful face not easily forgotten. Ngema phoned her whenever he had the chance (later, Thembela unknowingly placed the calls for him, until she caught on). A year after their first meeting, Xoliswa finished high school and returned to her family in Daveyton township, where Mtwa's family also lived. Ngema met her again when he and Mtwa were deported from the Transkei and moved to Daveyton. A year after that meeting, they were married in a private ceremony before a magistrate.

When Ngema's grandfather Vukayibambe first set eyes on Xoliswa, he regarded her with suspicion. Because the Xhosa and Zulu languages are very closely related, sharing a large common vocabulary, Zulu came easily to her. But to 110-year-old Vukayibambe, born a Zulu before the Zulu-British war, this educated, urbane young woman seemed like a foreigner and an exotic. "Who is this Shangaan?" he asked Ngema with consternation, categorizing her with what was probably the most alien South African ethnic group he could think of. "Do you trust her?"

Ma Hadebe's first words of advice to Xoliswa were to stay with her husband at all times—never trust him, never leave him alone. To keep Zwelikhethabantu in check, Ma Hadebe had found it necessary to travel with him wherever he went, even when the conditions were life-threatening—to the tent in Tugela Ferry in the cross fire of automatic rifles, to the men's barracks in Verulam. But still she had failed to prevent him from taking another wife, a woman called Ma Guneni, who lived in Ndwedwe, about an hour's drive south of Hlabisa. Ma Guneni had no children by Zwelikhethabantu and so hadn't sapped much of his money. He built her a small general store, which sustained her throughout her life. She required no further support.

In the traditional societies of South Africa, a man may marry as many women as his personal wealth will afford—and wealth is conferred upon a family through the marriage of its daughters. The engagement custom of *lobola,* a man's payment of a dowry to his fiancée's family, spans the various ethnic groupings and is one of the traditional practices most sturdily resistant to detribalization and dispersion. In the rural areas, *lobola* is still paid in cattle in an amount determined through formal, codified negotiations between the groom's and the bride's representatives. In the urban areas, it's usually paid in hard currency. The standard rate today is around 10,000 rand, but the amount is always negotiable. *Lobola,* in the words of Bessie Head, has "overtones of complete bondage . . . and undertones of a sales bargain."

Once *lobola* is paid, the woman is considered to be the man's wife, even though she will probably continue to live with her own family until after the formal wedding. If the couple chooses to comply with custom to the fullest extent, there will be many more rites to perform before the ultimate ceremony, which may not come for months or years—not infrequently, it doesn't come at all. If they break up before the wedding, it's considered bad luck for the man to ask for his *lobola* back.

Once married, the bride transfers her fealty to her husband's family and submits to the direct rule of her mother-in-law, whose command can be especially stringent in the rural areas. There a young wife will enjoy no honeymoon period with her new family; she will be put to work immediately, at the lowest level; her rise up the hierarchy of women, her new mothers and sisters, will be slow. When Xoliswa paid her first visit to Hlabisa as Ngema's wife, she was expected to cook and clean. She was accustomed to hard work—in her father's tiny house in Daveyton she had learned to cook for her family before she learned to read—but here she was expected to prepare meals in immense iron pots on kindling fires for a huge family; to serve the men upon her knees; to carry water from the river on her head; to *hlonipha* her in-laws by covering her hair and shoulders, keeping her eyes lowered bashfully, and never speaking unless spoken to. Xoliswa had a high school diploma, a distinction no Ngema could claim, and planned to go on to university. In Zululand, she was suddenly immersed in a tra-ditional way of life that was far more rigidly conservative than any fu-ture her urban upbringing—which could hardly be called indulgent or liberal—had prepared her for. The adjustments she had to make dur-ing those first family visits came with excruciating difficulty.

Although in the course of many stays in Hlabisa she eventually at-tained stature among the women and learned to adapt to rural life when she had to, she found it impossible to follow, unwaveringly, her mother-in-law's introductory advice. Ngema traveled a great deal throughout their marriage. Xoliswa had her own interests and respon-sibilities to keep her at home and wasn't always able to follow him, and she wasn't his only wife for long. Xoliswa is a college-educated woman with a natural brilliance and beauty, who has traveled widely and lives very much in the modern world, and yet she endured Ngema's other women for a number of years, grappling with conflicted and chaotic feelings. Her divorce from Ngema, recently finalized, was sought only after he had taken a second and a third wife.

The first years of their marriage were a busy and exciting time. When *Woza* went overseas in 1982, Xoliswa attended a university in Durban, visiting Ngema in the States or in Europe during her school breaks. In 1983, Ngema went back to South Africa between tours to assemble and train the *Asinamali!* company. When he de-parted to join *Woza* again, he left the *Asinamali!* actors in Xoliswa's care. She cooked their meals on a Primus stove and attended classes while the men—as many as ten at a time, until Ngema made the final cut—ran through their drills.

In 1986, Ngema and Xoliswa moved to a house in Daveyton, where they were immediately joined by the twenty teenagers who constituted the *Sarafina!* cast. At the age of twenty-four, Xoliswa became Mother Hubbard. To win the consent of the girls' parents, Ngema had made a vow that their daughters wouldn't be treated as domestic workers (as most of them were in their own homes) and that cooking and cleaning would be provided. Consequently, the girls felt entitled, for the first time in their lives, to make a mess. Xoliswa was constantly berating them to clean up after themselves—the boys, she says, did so without her urging. She superintended meals and laundry while Ngema ran his round-the-clock rehearsals in the backyard.

In 1987, after she received her undergraduate degree in social sciences, Xoliswa served in the official capacity of chief administrator of Committed Artists. She oversaw daily operations, which expanded enormously once Ngema sent *Sarafina!* overseas. In 1988, he held auditions for a second company, drawing hundreds of youngsters from all over the country, and doubled in number the Committed Artists family. While Ngema was in New York preparing to record two albums, Xoliswa transformed a warehouse in the Fordsburg area of Johannesburg into a new company headquarters, with dormitories, offices, and rehearsal space. Ngema underwrote a large portion of the cost personally, and the *Sarafina!* and *Asinamali!* companies were required to contribute a percentage of their weekly pay toward the upkeep and expansion of the facility. Xoliswa untangled the confusion of erratic incoming funds, kept the place in order, and moderated the personal conflicts that constantly arose among the shifting band of actors. In 1990, Ngema opened *Township Fever* with a company of fifty and then made a million-rand sound-track recording of the show, which drained the company's and Ngema's personal accounts. During the lean time that followed, Xoliswa managed to scrape together the utility payments and to fend off the landlord each month. She had an integral role in Ngema's life and was well positioned to observe, as it evolved, the relationship he developed with the young woman who would be his second wife, Leleti Khumalo, the star of *Sarafina!*

A number of South African men have complained to me that South African women are mercenary when it comes to romance, that they won't even glance at a man who has no steady income. But Ngema's example seems to refute this generalization. While today many poverty-stricken parents would be thrilled to confer their daughters on a man as prosperous as Ngema, regardless of how many wives he already has, it is also true that he has never been without female companionship, not even when he was destitute. Even in his most desperately insolvent hours he nearly always had at least one woman willing to shelter him, feed him, tend to his laundry, and fortify his ego and his heart with her love. He freely acknowledges that he could not have survived any of his periods of homelessness and poverty without the women who cared for him.

Today he is fastidious about his meals and his wardrobe, but he is absolutely incapable—or so he protests—of cooking his dinner, ironing his shirts, or packing his suitcase.

When she met Ngema, Khumalo was a shy, skinny girl from a troubled, single-parent home in KwaMashu township, near Durban. As a member of a dancing and singing club, she sang on a minor record Ngema made in early 1985. A year later, when he assembled a cast for *Sarafina!,* he looked to the girls from that club. By then Khumalo had become a radiant beauty with an intense quality; in real life she was painfully bashful, but in rehearsals she had a Zen-like ability to enter, fearlessly, the spiritual world of the play and revealed astonishing gifts as an actress. She was still excruciatingly shy in the presence of journalists and foreign producers, but for six years, performing in South Africa, New York, across America, and in South Africa again, she attacked her role onstage with courage and assurance and never missed a performance. In 1992, she adjusted her acting style to play Sarafina in the motion picture adaptation of the play and gave a stunning performance. And by then her comportment before the paparazzi was graceful, secure, and natural.

Khumalo grew up under Ngema's tutelage. Throughout their long hours of work together, she became deeply attached to him. As she matured, they fell in love. Some years ago, he paid *lobola.* In 1990, he bought a house for her in the white suburb of Bryanston, near Johannesburg, and began spending most of his time there. At Christmastime, 1991, when he was still married to Xoliswa and maintaining their home in Daveyton, he formally married Khumalo in an unusual Christian ceremony in Durban, followed by a reception at the five-star Holiday Inn on the Marine Parade (not far from the hotels where it had

been Ngema's fondest aspiration, some fourteen years before, to perform for whites for loose change). Then a reported two thousand
people converged on the farm in Hlabisa for further celebrations.

The major newspapers had been following the wedding preparations for weeks, focusing on the polygamy. While it was openly tolerated in the rural areas, the practice was usually kept under wraps in the
cities; Ngema's openness about his plans for a second marriage was
scandalously controversial. The reports following the wedding were
even more sensational. In a full-color photo—nine by seven and a half
inches—of the newlyweds on the front page of the *Sunday Times,*
Khumalo is radiant in a conventional white gown frosted with lace and
satin, with clusters of pearls on her ears, a long strand of pearls knot-
ted around her neck, and a chaste veil over her head; Ngema is fash-
ionably casual in a brown-and-gold batik-print jacket over a gold silk
shirt, unbuttoned at the neck. "High Drama at Showbiz Wedding,"
the headline reads. The producer of the *Sarafina!* film, Anant Singh,
was there, along with Hugh Masekela and many more entertainment
personalities, who "looked on in amazement when the grand wedding
they attended did not take place."

Xoliswa Ngema had retained a lawyer, the report goes on, who sent
a fax that very morning advising the church that Ngema was already legally married. The white clergyman, who had been innocent of this information, was shaken by the news and retired to his chambers for
seventy-five minutes of private soul-searching. Finally, Ngema's supporters convinced him to proceed with the service. Hugh Masekela
summoned the guests into the church to witness a hurried, provisional
benediction. It was not the service they'd planned, but afterward, the
couple were satisfied enough to beam for the cameras.

▼

In April 1990, a year and a half before the wedding to Khumalo and
nine years after he married Xoliswa, Ngema took me on a drive to
Mahlabatini, a Zulu village adjoining Ulundi—the capital of the
KwaZulu homeland and seat of Gatsha Buthelezi's Inkatha Freedom
Party—to witness his payment of *lobola* for a third wife, the sixteen-
year-old Cebisila. Three of his brothers were serving as his represen-

tatives in this matter. Ngema wasn't required to be there, but he wanted to see his sixteen head of cattle merging with the herd of Cebi's father—a man endowed, by most estimates, with sixteen wives of his own and a fortune in marriageable daughters. Ngema has inherited a rapturous love for cows from his grandfather, and he enjoys pointing out the beautifully built and marked ones that straggle, most of them miserably and hungrily, in the parched back roads of Zululand. At the time, he was experiencing a rediscovery of his traditional culture and ancestral landscape.

In Pongola, on the Natal border, we encountered a roadblock and a scornful white policeman, who tore apart our luggage in the trunk and found my diary, which he read from cover to cover, scanning the lines with one finger in the Evelyn Wood style. Stuck between the pages he found a magazine that featured on its cover a color photo of Ngema. He gaped at the photo, turned to study Ngema's face, and then returned to my diary with redoubled vigor. "That's very personal," I finally found the words to say, as one who has compulsively hidden her journals from parents and roommates all her life. "I have a right to do this, you know," he said. "This isn't America." Ngema stood by stoically, as one who had been through far worse than this many times. Finally, finding nothing subversive, steamy, or, I suspect, even scrutable in my diary, the policeman let us go.

Ngema drove at a steady 120–140 kph as we crossed the wall of the Drakensberg Mountains into Natal, zigzagging and corkscrewing our way toward Mahlabatini. The sky darkened with a foreshadowing of rain. For miles and miles at a time, we would cling to a mountain and could see nothing but rock and stubble, the cows and goats that wandered stupidly into our path, and quiet settlements of mud-and-thatch rondavels. And then the landscape would suddenly bottom out. Teetering on a ledge, we could see columns of rain angling from the sky into distant, tiny villages. At one such vantage point, Ngema said, "That's where we're going," and gestured toward the darkest, farthest shaft and the stormiest miniature settlement. And then the mountain rapidly enclosed us again.

Shortly before nightfall, when we finally arrived in Mahlabatini, it was pouring. We were swept from the car, across an expanse of mud, and into the small house inhabited by Cebisila's older brother, an actor in the second company of *Sarafina!* and the agent of this union, nicknamed Senzavsky (an amalgam of Senzangakona, one of his favorite Zulu kings, and Stanislavsky, his favorite dramatic theorist). The house was a small rectangle divided into three tiny rooms. Ngema's brothers were already in the center room, slouched over on the three-piece red velvet parlor suite—which Senzavsky bought with his *Sarafina!* savings—and murmuring in the low tones of Zulu social intercourse, waiting for the dark to descend. The rain pounded away at the tin roof. A young girl in a tattered dress blew in, fell to her knees, and crawled to Ngema and me with a dish of water, which she held steadily as we rinsed our hands in turn. Soon a young boy, similarly frayed and threadbare, entered the house with lukewarm soda pop and two glasses, and served our beverages from his knees. Another young girl entered, with heaping dishes of chicken, beans, and rice domed by inverted plates, carried on trays shrouded with colorful doilies. Through the raucous drumming on the roof we heard the high-pitched wails and ululations of the elder women who were outside, receiving Ngema's cattle. Candles were lit, and the hushed colloquium took on a dreamlike haze.

The bride herself was conspicuously absent from the gathering. Her father and mother, prevented by custom from sitting with their future son-in-law, were also missing. The group gathered in this house were roughly of Senzavsky's generation and younger. Children crept in and curled up on straw mats in the corners of the center room until they were displaced by elders who had been displaced by *their* elders out of elevated seats. Before long, the small children were all crowded in an adjoining room and listening through an open doorway. Then they became bored. One of their senior members began to tell stories, to which they listened with rapt, unblinking fascination.

To attend the big feast the next day, many of Cebisila's family members traveled long distances from the cities where they worked. Cebi's father presented a sheep to the senior brother among Ngema's representatives and then instructed his sons to slaughter it. As they slid the knife softly into its neck, the animal let out a forgiving, fatalistic bleat; blood jetted from the wound and into a dish. I spent most of the day in the rectangular house with Ngema, receiving meals and making friends. At one point, Ngema turned to me with a look of absolute peace and contentedness and said, "You sit and wait to see who's going to come through the door next, and whoever it is, it will be good."

Finally, Cebisila sneaked in shyly while her elders were preoccupied elsewhere and flashed her loveliest qualities: a brilliant, easy smile, a sweet, soft voice, and a dazzling poise, which she'd acquired recently, I think, with the boon of her enviable engagement. When one of her mothers—any of her father's sixteen wives—came by, she quietly vanished again.

The kraal of Cebi's father consists mostly of the typical round, dank mud huts with thatched roofs, one for each wife and her children. A couple of the older, senior sons, who have married or have earned their own money, have built their own houses. Only a few of the huts are rectangular in shape—one of them is the communal kitchen, where, when they weren't cooking, the mamas could be found singing and crooning, "Awu! Hayi! Awu!" and dancing, heavily, beneath the weight of their bosoms. Whenever one of the mamas came to visit with us in the rectangular house, she removed her shoes and pointed her eyes directly at the mat in the corner, where she immediately lowered herself upon cushiony legs. She would always wait to be greeted before venturing to say hello. When she was invited to speak, she did so with her eyes lowered girlishly. When Cebi's own birth-mother came to Ngema to formally discuss her daughter's future, she addressed him from the floor, on hands and knees, her center of gravity swaying midway between her shoulders and her hips. Ngema, though high up in the superior position on the velvet sofa, tendered her a reciprocal, bashful, filial respect, nodding and agreeing: "Eh heh, eh heh." Their eyes never met.

In this kraal, Ngema had an uncommon role—he was both a respectful son-in-law and a venerated messiah, by whose grace Senzavsky had toured the world and earned the money to build this house. Many long-held customs were being stretched and bent for Ngema, though with no great strain. Accommodations were made for me too— the eldest father invited me to stay at Ngema's elbow in places where only men were customarily admitted, and treated me as if I were one of Ngema's brothers. Graciousness and flexibility seemed to come naturally here, in spite of the stiff Zulu protocol.

Later that night, a young boy entered Senzavsky's house bearing a wooden platter heaped with the most delectable organs of the sacrificial beast—liver, intestines, heart, tongue—which he carved into bite-size morsels. The honored guests and ranking elder men reached in and took with their hands, while the younger people held back. Then Cebi's father, the patriarch of all present, entered the house. He was a wiry man, half the size of any of his wives, with long-hanging looped earlobes. Ngema was obliged to segregate himself, and I joined him in the little partitioned room east of center, where we could watch and listen through an open door. A boy brought us our own platter of meat and *jega* (bread steamed like a dumpling) and our own drinks. The rest of the house filled up beyond reasonable capacity. Night fell and candles were lit. Soon all the children were dislodged from the house, and although it had begun to drizzle, they watched from outside, pressing their faces against the only window. The mothers and adult daughters filled the room to the west of center so tightly that they could only stand. The center room was occupied exclusively by men. The oldest of them and Ngema's brothers sat on the few pieces of furniture. Those who were younger covered the floor, leaving only a small clearing in the middle, and passed around a clay pot of home-brewed beer. One man began to sing, and the others instantly formed a chorus and answered him, clapping a steady, heavy rhythm. One by one the men took their turns dancing in a meditative, high-kicking style in the small clear space. The women were dancing too, but they could only jump directly up and down, en masse. "Awu, my son!" they cried to the featured dancer as his foot sledgehammered down onto the floor in a rhythmic convulsion. The women's voices joined the chorus too, faintly at first, then gaining confidence and swelling, and then branching off into their own distinct melody; soon there were two independent, contrapuntal strains of equal force, one on top of the other, bouncing off the tin roof and entwining like two joined hands. Manifest in the extended arms and lifted chins and raised voices of those inside the circle was pure joy.

"We believe," Steve Biko wrote, "that in the long run the special contribution to the world by Africa will be in this field of human relationship. The great powers of the world may have done wonders in giving the world an industrial and military look, but the great gift still has to come from Africa—giving the world a more human face."[2]

Escorted by members of her family, Cebisila has visited Ngema's home in Bryanston on a number of occasions. Ngema claims that she and Khumalo get along well and enjoy each other's company, though that remains to be seen. In the meantime, Ngema and Khumalo continue to flourish together creatively. When Cebi is finished with her schooling, the three may live together under one roof, though the details of the future arrangements remain unsettled. Meanwhile, Ngema is living out his most traditional inclinations, and the protracted sequence of prewedding rituals has advanced. I recently saw a photo of Cebisila from a ceremony more formal than the one I witnessed: Caught in a moment of splendor, noble-chinned, bare-breasted, in traditional garb made of reeds, skins, and beads, a cone-shaped hat on her head, she is seated on the ground, her legs folded demurely to her side. And upon her feet she wears brand-new American jogging shoes.

Chapter Twelve

▼

The least I can ever say for myself is that I forcefully created for myself, under extremely hostile conditions, my ideal life.

BESSIE HEAD[1]

Ngema's Bryanston residence, a pinkish Spanish-style ranch house, named Casa Rio by previous owners, is tucked behind an old-fashioned iron gate—the last of its kind in a neighborhood taken over by electronic security devices—on a street so quiet after ten o'clock at night that the clink of two keys against his doorknob excites the howls of enormous-sounding dogs in homes a block away. Behind the house there's a tiled patio and a kidney-shaped swimming pool, beyond which the landscape dips, then flattens out at a broad expanse of green lawn, and dips again into a lighted, sunken tennis court with the acoustics of a rock quarry. Tall trees in a row guard the back of the property like sentinels. Standing there, one can very clearly hear the gentle gurgling of the little *rio* that grazes the border on the other side.

Ngema bought the house in early 1990, a year and a half before the repeal of the Group Areas Act, which he circumvented by forming a close corporation with two white friends, a lawyer and a theater producer, who merely signed their names to a deed; the black-run African Bank provided the mortgage; and the Group Areas Police were none the wiser. The price was about $160,000, around a tenth of what the same property would go for in a comparably up-scale American suburb. Even considering the real value of the rand, it can still be said that white wealth in South Africa has been a fantastic bargain.

It's very plain to see, however, that Bryanston is not an American suburb; it's a white enclave in black Africa. Affordable and abundant, the black domestic workers and all their hangers-on surely outnumber by far the town's legitimate residents. While the whites zip in and out of their electronic gates in Mercedeses and BMWs, the blacks who work in Bryanston travel largely by foot and are always visible trekking the residential lanes or working on strangely silent building sites, performing by hand the kind of labor done by raucous machines in other countries. Ngema and the miniature, isolated Zulu community he has installed at Casa Rio exist among them in perfect camouflage.

While the lady of the house, Khumalo, was on tour with *Sarafina!*, rotating shifts of Ngema's women relatives took up residence to tend to his cooking and cleaning. Today as always, women sweep the wall-to-wall carpeting with a small brush, on their knees, and wash the laundry by hand. The family sometimes eats together at a table in the kitchen. But Ngema usually takes his meals on the red velvet sofa in the living room; the woman serving him usually does so upon her knees, as in Hlabisa.

The house was originally built for a small family of approximately four—gracious and comfortable, but far from a mansion. Now it's always overcrowded with Ngema's extended family. There are usually two or three people to a bed, and others on sofas in the parlor and the den. But the housekeepers are so fastidious and thorough in their work, and the inhabitants so organized and sensible in their personal habits, that there is never any disorder. An early-morning visitor would never guess that so many people are living there. The floors are washed and swept every day, and silently—the hardworking force of women make it seem to happen by magic.

I have never seen anyone swim or play tennis at Casa Rio. Occasionally in residence is a gaggle of small boys, Ngema's nephews, who make use of the pool by playing a running game around it, the objective of which is to not fall in. Other games of chasing, dancing, and mock fighting are played on the tennis court. From the row of tall trees, Ngema has chosen the tallest as the one beneath which he makes his daily prayers to his ancestors. Although few of the amenities function as they were originally intended, everything is used and nothing is taken for granted. On either side of the property live white families who swim, play tennis, and hire gardeners to prune their trees and maids to do the vacuuming, and whose children have private bedrooms. But the women who care for Ngema still undertake housekeeping as a skilled profession, and they endow his house with a feeling of extraordinary luxury. After so many years of homelessness, Ngema takes his home seriously. When he is far away, he longs to return to Casa Rio. He loves every square inch of it.

The irony of his choice to make his primary residence in a fancy white suburb, after earning his fame by raising his voice against the white oppressor and demanding a "new South Africa," wouldn't be lost on James Baldwin, who wrote:

> It must be remembered that the oppressed and the oppressor are bound together within the same society; they accept the same criteria . . . they both alike depend on the same reality. Within this cage it is romantic, more, meaningless, to speak of a "new" society as the desire of the oppressed. . . . What is meant by a new society is one in which inequalities will disappear . . . either there will be no oppressed at all, or the oppressed and the oppressor will change places. But, finally, as it seems to me, what the rejected desire is, is an elevation of status, acceptance within the present community.[2]

Ngema bought the house immediately before the Market Theatre premiere of *Township Fever,* which he'd been developing and rehearsing for nearly two years, and he moved in just a few days before Nelson Mandela was released from prison. Ngema's previous plays had been generally embraced by the leaders of the foremost anti-apartheid movements, his success widely viewed as a positive advance for all black South Africans. Although he'd never joined the ANC or any political party, Winnie Mandela had always come out to support his work. But just before the opening of *Township Fever,* the government lifted the ban on the ANC and other groups, which then quickly splintered into special-interest factions scrambling to reserve their new acronyms and establish their positions of power. Ngema and his work came under new, harsh scrutiny.

Township Fever has the makings of a classically structured epic, a *Romeo and Juliet* centered around a true-life tragedy of immense proportions and profound significance to the ANC. In 1987, some twenty thousand black employees of the state-owned railway system, SATS, went on strike to protest a number of outrageous abuses and insults, demobilizing the railways and costing the government millions of rand in lost revenues. SATS management responded by firing the strikers and ordering them to vacate their hostels and return to their ethnic homelands. Then government forces besieged a union meeting, killing three strikers. Armed only with spears and knobkerries, members of the union marched through the streets of Johannesburg to confront the police and the army. In the melee that ensued, five more men were killed. The frustration and fury spiraling within the union could find no outlet, so it turned inward, against workers who had defied the strike. At a meeting at the headquarters of Cosatu (the labor union federation now openly allied with the ANC), the majority voted to execute five scabs. One of the scabs managed to escape and later collaborated with the police. But four others were killed, and eighteen men were arrested and charged with the murders. Later, confounded by a protracted nationwide campaign of massive stay-aways and train boycotts, SATS reinstated the strikers and agreed to meet their demands.

Ngema's lawyer, David Dison, was a member of the legal team that defended the eighteen accused killers in court. He provided Ngema with transcripts and documents and took him to Pretoria Central Prison to meet the men who had been convicted of the murders, still lingering on death row. Through a two-year-long process of plotting, composing, and rehearsing with thirty actors, Ngema pieced together an enormous work that held within its three and a half hours everything that was of interest to him.

His protagonist, a young man named Jazz, is a talented composer and musician who lives in a Soweto shantytown called Mshenguville with his widowed mother. Jazz wants to marry a beautiful girl, Tonko, who is from a slightly more affluent family, also headed by a widow. Tonko's domineering mother abhors the idea of her daughter marrying a poor, unemployed boy like Jazz. Jazz wishes only to write his music and resists entering the labor force, but his desire to marry Tonko is overpowering, and he finally takes a job that will enable him to support her. His best friend, Philadelphia, works at SATS and helps to find him a position there. Ironically, in order to marry Tonko, Jazz must be separated from her, and he moves into a single-men's hostel, where he soon becomes embroiled in the strike and in an outrage that recasts his life. He is one of the men inculpated in the scab murders. His best friend, Philadelphia, is the informer who fingers him.

In the real-life trial, Dison and his colleagues tried to prove that their clients had been dehumanized by a situation of intense conflict—in every attribute a war—that had soared out of their control. Accordingly, Ngema saw Jazz and his comrades, who were driven by circumstance to commit murder, as victims. But he didn't look for easy answers or unexamined outrage. He wrote a scene that gave the scabs a chance to make heart-rending pleas for their lives. They cried that they had to work in order to feed their children, to pay hospital bills for their loved ones.

Ngema wrote in the program: "I was fascinated by the idea that people without any criminal record could be compelled to commit gruesome acts totally out of character with their personalities." To show the true personalities of men accused as murderers, he offered exuberant and extravagantly produced musical numbers illustrating their lives outside of SATS. The elaborately staged wedding of Tonko and Jazz took up nearly an hour of performance time, without advancing the plot, and could have stood on its own as a folk ballet.

Shortly after the opening, I interviewed Mzwakhe Mbuli, known popularly as Mzwakhe, the People's Poet, a superstar oral poet in his early thirties. Over the years, he had been banned, detained, tortured, and repeatedly denied a passport. At the time, he was heading up Cosatu's so-called Cultural Desk in Johannesburg and was at the forefront of a movement to boycott *Township Fever.*

Mbuli showed me the minutes of that week's meeting of the Cultural Desk's council. High up on the list of topics discussed was "Mbongeni Ngema," followed by an itemization of the complaints against him, including an accusation that he'd co-opted, for his own commercial gain, a major event in the people's struggle and, secondarily, allegations of his womanizing, the latter a charge the Desk never, to my knowledge, pursued.

"The ideas that Mbongeni has," Mbuli told me, "are not ideas that are *creatively* conceived. It's material that is already there, ushered by our struggles." Mbuli said he had admired *Asinamali!* and *Sarafina!* In *Township Fever,* however, Ngema had attempted something he hadn't tried before. It seemed that what was so upsetting to many people about the play was not that he'd commercialized a communal tragedy so much as that he'd *personalized* it. He took the enormous SATS strike of 1987 and adapted it to his own life. He wrote a play about a musician, like himself, with a delicate sensibility, who must run from one impossibly hostile situation to another and, in Jazz's case, engage in acts of violence contrary to his nature. Ngema tried to show that political commitment exacts dear costs in terms of human feelings and love. The play seems less political than personal, aiming at a more private kind of spiritual enlightenment.

But "[p]rivate emotions," wrote Nadine Gordimer some years earlier, "were inevitably outlawed by political activists who had no time for any."[3] Ngema invested himself, in the most personal way, in his play, bestowing his characters with his own compassion and luxuriating in his own contradictions; Mbuli, who had always been too busy fighting a regime to exorcise his private emotions through his art, wrote poems meant to promote resistance, to publicly mourn, to unite with stirring chants and rhythms.

Banners advertising *Township Fever* were torn down in the townships. On the commuter trains, comrades chanted against the play and exhorted people to stay away from it. Meetings were held among Cosatu's leadership, its Living Wage group, and shop stewards from SARHWU—the railway workers union behind the 1987 strike—as well as among members of the fledgling Theatre Alliance of the Transvaal, to harmonize their denunciation.

Ngema attended a meeting called by the national leadership of the Cosatu Cultural Desk and addressed, point by point, the complaints raised against him. It was charged that the union meetings had been improperly depicted in the play as scenes of disorder, brawling, and drunkenness; a scene showing a witch doctor anointing the strikers before their Johannesburg march was demeaning and anachronistic; the detailed description of the brutal scab murders was delivered so graphically that it might "kill the morale of the people to fight the state," as one critic said.

Some took offense at the buffoonery of rustic characters Ngema inserted into the workers' hostel for comic relief. Others took umbrage at the lyric "All the politicians are corrupt/All the governments of this world are corrupt," with its implication that ANC politicians must also be corrupt. "The play doesn't bring hope," one detractor told me. Because Ngema freely used the actual names of the organizations involved in the strike, and of Mandela, some ANC affiliates felt licensed to censure and expected Ngema to make amends. Many wanted him to rewrite the play.

This he absolutely would not do. In the past, he had always taken criticism well; parlaying a few grains of outside opinion into a major innovation is one of his greatest skills. He's that rare theater person who actually looks forward to reading his reviews for helpful suggestions. But this time he was truly inflamed by external judgment. He was consumed by the affront and raged about it constantly. For the meeting with the Cultural Desk, however, he cooled off and calmly presented wall charts and thick files of collected research to support his claims to the facts presented in *Township Fever.*

In the end, no formal boycott ever materialized, and no changes were made in the script. Many within Cosatu and the ANC, including Nelson Mandela, supported Ngema. There were some subsequent evenings when the theater was filled with SARHWU shop stewards with ANC green, black, and gold epaulets pinned to their shoulders, scribbling notes in the dark, and evenings when the auditorium, for unknown reasons, was only half full. But the play had closed and moved to New York before any consensus of protest could be reached.

Around the time of the Johannesburg opening, Albie Sachs, a leading ANC intellectual, delivered a paper—which his comrade Mbuli didn't much care for—proposing that "members should be banned from saying that culture is a weapon of struggle" for a period of five years. Ngema was gratified to hear:

In the case of a real instrument of the struggle, there is no room for ambiguity: a gun is a gun is a gun, and if it were full of contradictions, it would fire in all sorts of directions and be useless for its purpose. . . . If we had the imagination of Sholokhov, and one of us wrote *And Quiet Flows the Tugela,* the central figure would not be a member of UDF or Cosatu, but would be aligned to Inkatha, resisting change, yet feeling oppression, thrown this way and that by conflicted emotions, and through his or her struggles and torments and moments of joy, the reader would be thrust into the whole drama of the struggle for a new South Africa.

Because the majority of black South Africans have been deliberately kept semiliterate at best, if there were a South African Sholokhov, his books would reach only an elite group. Theater artists like Ngema and oral poets like Mzwakhe therefore carry an enormous burden. They alone are in a position to communicate not just political slogans and sentiment but real *feeling* to the masses.

Finally, it may have been because he fell short of his ability that Ngema's claim to the raw material of *Township Fever* was so strenuously disputed. There was some justified artistic criticism circulating too: he may have devoted too much energy to the music and not enough to the script, which badly needed editing. A few critics suggested that he should have delegated some of the work to collaborators. He took twenty-one months to painstakingly research and write the play, to compose and orchestrate the music, to direct the actors—he had no critical distance from any aspect of it. He was hurt when so many people responded coldly—alone, he carried the full weight of the production. But that's the way he had wanted it. The title page of the Market Theatre program for *Township Fever* read:

ENTIRE PRODUCTION
Book, Music & Lyrics,
Conceived, Choreographed,
Musical Arrangements, Orchestration and
Direction by–
MBONGENI NGEMA

Ngema has always known intuitively, as Kenneth Tynan once said of Orson Welles, that "in show business, being inhibited gets you nowhere." He has never been embarrassed about taking credit and seeking the limelight. Barney Simon says Ngema is like a cancer: "It destroys, but it's a life force. You can't stop it from being what it is."

There are no lapses into philosophic boredom for Ngema, no ennui. He's far more likely to suffer from his excesses than from any hollow-ness or nihilism. He can drink too much, spend too much, work too hard, react too strongly. He'll read a newspaper article about gang-sters, somewhere in South Africa, hurling people from moving com-muter trains or, somewhere else, schoolchildren setting people aflame, and he will turn to whoever is beside him and ask, not at all rhetori-cally but hoping despairingly for a reasonable response: "How can we stop this? Why does it happen?"

What enraptures him now are the facets of his country that he's known all his life: the swooning, head-spinning, voluptuous forms of the Natal mountainscape, a well-built cow, music (most of all his own), wedding feasts, the faces and forms of pretty women, and idiosyncratic people in all walks of South African life. He is not happy when he is not in South Africa.

He never forgets the hostile conditions out of which he made his ideal life, and he prays daily, if his schedule allows. He would not pre-sume to appeal to God directly; the ancestors are his intermediaries.

Prayer is the starting point for his rehearsals too. And whenever his actors seem to be getting coddled into temperamental excesses or laziness on the stage—whether in New York or London or Johannes-burg—he reminds them of who they are and where they've come from. After a disappointing performance of *Township Fever*, he was furious and scolded the company. "I've built my name," he said. "People re-spect my work. But you don't have credibility yet. This cast can be changed tomorrow. There can be totally new people, but it will still be *Township Fever*, so you'd better take it very seriously. Think of our fa-thers who work in the gold mines, miles underground, all day, squat-ting, digging gold, earning money for their children. You're not in a factory or in the mines, you're not in Zululand, plowing. You can't stand onstage and give your full commitment for two and a half hours? You must work like the miners, the same amount of energy, dedica-tion, and will. You must say, 'It's my only mission in life.' "

CHAPTER THIRTEEN

▼

We are always lost in our crowds, our human value nullified.
MTUTUZELI MATSHOBA[1]

Sadly, neither Ngema's parents nor his grandfather lived to see his Bryanston home. At the age of 116, Vukayibambe died a natural death. Zwelikhethabantu passed away in 1982 at the age of sixty, eight years after he was stricken with his debilitating illness. In spite of her husband's rigid religious taboos, Ma Hadebe pursued every remedy available to him, although many advances in modern medicine were out of their reach. Because there is no hospital in Hlabisa, Ma Hadebe had to transport him to Durban to see overburdened doctors, who never had, or took, the time to explain what had happened to him or to offer any real prognosis or hope. She took him to *inyangas* and spiritualists, who supplied him with arcane remedies derived from tree roots and herbs, or prescribed supernatural cures, to no discernible effect.

In 1985, three years after her husband's death, Ma Hadebe began suffering from incapacitating headaches and chronic lassitude. She went to a doctor in Durban, who gave her a routine physical examination and told her she had a brain tumor, which required immediate surgery. Because the African hospital wasn't equipped to perform the procedure, Ma Hadebe was transferred to an Indian hospital for the operation and then moved directly back for recovery. Three weeks later, Ngema visited her and, finding her looking well, decided that it

the way I was rubbing him in the car and he revived. He became himself. But the doctor said, "Okay, I'll admit him. Take him to the admission ward."

I left him there. He was just fine. "Okay, Ndaba," I said, "I'll see you in the evening." But unfortunately, the nurses told me, we're not allowed to visit patients at night because people come and murder, you know. "So," I said, "I'll see you on Tuesday." That was on Sunday. "Anyway, I'll keep on ringing."

Sunday evening I phoned: "How is Ndaba?"

"Oh, he is fine," the nurse said. "He's sleeping."

Monday morning at six I phoned. They said, "He's still sleeping. Otherwise he's fine."

At lunchtime, at one, I phoned again. I asked them, "Did he eat?"

They said, "He ate, but the food came out. He vomited."

I asked, "How do you think he is?"

"He's fine. He's been dancing all over. He's been busy in the ward. Nobody's sleeping in the ward. You know how your husband is. He's making these comedy films of his in the ward."

They don't allow you to talk to the patients. In the evening I phoned again. The nurse said, "My dear, he's just stumped. His eyes are opened but he doesn't say a word. But he's still alive."

Tuesday morning at eight, I phoned again. "How is Ndaba's condition?"

They said, "Are you Mary?"

"Yes, Ndaba's wife. Yes."

"Ask somebody to come with you to the hospital."

I said, "Why?" Because the way we were so together with Ndaba, every time of our life, I thought, maybe Ndaba's made a trick. He's missing me. He wants to see me. I know he's jocular. He wants to say something. He wants to be with me. Yet, "Why?"

"But please, Mary, come with somebody."

No one at the hospital could tell Twala how her husband had died. And it didn't occur to her to push for an explanation. Mhlongo was a celebrated actor, a stage and television star, fresh from Broadway, but he didn't receive even mediocre care, which surprised no one.

Illness is a terrible pit for a black South African to fall into. Seriously sick people usually stay sick and live fatalistically, untreated, until they die. And fatigue, which can invite sickness, must be fended off with the extreme vigilance of the Zulu migrant workers I saw once, dancing in a delirious high-kicking style outside their Soweto hostel, just moments before a wave of violence ensnaring Inkatha and the ANC deluged the Johannesburg area. They told me that they were dancing instead of resting on their one day off from work in order to "get rid of their fatigue."

In 1990, Ignatia, the Pimville widow with whom Ngema once stayed, finally got very tired of Soweto and gave up on it. A group of strange men had ganged up on another man, stabbed him, and left him for dead in the street just before her house. But the victim was alive—he dragged himself, spewing hot blood, across Ignatia's front yard, across her threshold, through her living room, and into her bed. His attackers returned to the scene, followed his trail into the house, hauled him out of bed, and finished him off on the front stoop. Later, the killers were arrested. Ignatia hadn't witnessed the murder, but because it had been committed on her property, she was required to attend the trial in Johannesburg every day for months. This ordeal, finally, defeated her. When it was over, all she wanted was to leave Soweto, where she'd battled sedulously for calm her entire adult life, and give way to her fatigue on a dry patch of exhausted land in her ancestral home in Zululand.

Many of the other people in Ngema's life are just where he left them. Margaret from Umlazi is in her eighties now, living in the same senior citizens home where she volunteered her services for so many years. She still has her vigor, her delicate bearing, and her weakness for young artists—there's a certain church choir that she's been championing lately. Her daughter, the Zulu Shirley Temple, is now a grandmother and, like the eponymous, un-Zulu Shirley Temple, who retains little today of her childhood razzmatazz, a woman of sober responsibility.

▼

Mafiki is still in Clermont, married to the man she left Ngema for. She is presently a self-employed businesswoman, selling women's clothing door to door all day, every day. She says she has never punched a clock and never will. She lives in a compound of separate little one-room houses. Her room is clean and pleasant, with a hot plate for cooking, pictures on the walls, and comfortable furniture. Her daughter wants to be an actress, she tells me. And she, too, would secretly like to act again. If she had stayed with Ngema, she realizes now, she might have had the chance to travel overseas. But her present husband, who was then her fiancé, wouldn't have allowed it.

▼

Khassi and Bongi are well. They have just finished paying off the bond on their furniture. As soon as it was made legal for them to own their house outright, Khassi went to the bank and applied for a mortgage. He's still employed at the dry-cleaning company where he's worked for twenty-five years. Bongi is a nurse in the same maternity ward, where there's such a shortage of beds that many pregnant women must abide their final hours of labor on the floor; an average of fifty babies are delivered there every day. After many years on the night shift, she was recently transferred to days and can enjoy, at last, the luxury of spending her evenings with her family. She and Khassi recently celebrated their twenty-fifth wedding anniversary and now have two children, whom they adore—the first, a boy named Talent, was born immediately after Ngema left them to go to Gibson Kente in 1979. When I first visited them, Bongi brought out a huge platter heaped with home-baked pastries that looked as if they'd come out of a children's fantasy book— oversized cupcakes and cookies lacquered with surreal pink and chocolate icing, shiny and dense, far too beautiful to eat—and a second platter loaded with many kinds of fresh fruit.

Khassi doesn't drink as he did when Ngema was around, and he's resigned himself, at last, to the life of a fully grown and responsible man. He's learned from his past mistakes and recklessness, and he entertains no more dreams of showbiz triumph. But the couple are still in frequent contact with Ngema and share with him, more than ever, a feeling of true kinship. "I never heard of someone who did what I did," Khassi says wistfully. "I think I liked Mbongeni the first day I met him. I understood the business, and I was right inside—involved! It was a brave thing, a step forward. You know, to sponsor and to be involved are two different things. When you are involved, it's a part of you. If you sit down with Mbongeni, he'll say, 'You know, I've learned a lot from a man—Khassi.' Hey, too many plays we've been through with Mbongeni and tried so many things! But there are certain years one must do this, certain years one must do that. And we're still building our future, still planning our future."

▼

A short time after he briefly materialized to squelch Ngema's plans for *Too Harsh,* Lucky announced his engagement. All the arrangements were made for the wedding in Nqutu, and the *lobola* was paid. But on the day of the ceremony, Lucky disappeared again, this time fleeing the country altogether. His family reported that his defection had been provoked by political considerations. Lucky's best friend, who was like a brother to him, stepped in and married the woman in his place, as a brother is bound to do in Zulu custom when another is killed in war or goes away.

▼

Thembela still lives in the Transkei, is still unmarried, and until a short time ago was still working at the post office in Port St. Johns. She despised that job, by then, with all her heart.

Ngema tells me that he will always feel deeply indebted to Thembela. And it may be that she will always love him. When Ngema married Xoliswa, he had neither the heart nor the courage to tell Thembela. But when Thembela called as usual from the post office, she found out for herself: Xoliswa answered the phone in the unmistakable tone of a wife. Thembela was crushed, but today she says she has no ill feelings and doesn't regret the sacrifices she made for him: "Well, it is not right to support a man, especially if it's not your husband. But I felt that Mbongeni wanted to get what he was hoping to get at the end, and I felt, well, let me just help where I can. It was nothing that he was forcing me to do. I felt it was a way of giving moral support."

▼

Mali Hlatswayo, Dixon Malele, and Makalo Mofokeng have been working with Ngema steadily for years. Bra Vusi, who underwrote

Woza Albert! rehearsals, was unable to witness Ngema's success until late 1992, when he was released from a long prison sentence for bank robbery.

When I was in the Transkei in 1991, the Matanzima brothers were both in jail. Unseated by General Bantu Holomisa, stripped of their wealth, banned as enemies of the state, they were sent to serve terms in the very prison where they'd confined Ngema.

In a terrific stroke of serendipity, one day while Ngema was still performing in *Woza Albert!* in Johannesburg, he ran into a fellow who looked strikingly familiar. On closer examination, he saw that it was Skhumbuzo, the young boy he used to play music with in the aluminum factory, when neither of them had a job, a cent, or a home. Skhumbuzo was a man now, playing professionally with Ngema's friends The Soul Brothers, the most popular *mbaqanga* group in the country. Later, when Ngema assembled a band for the second company of *Sarafina!,* he hired Skhumbuzo to play guitar and kept him steadily employed for years.

Thandi Zulu is still saving children from the street and writing plays, although her original project, *Thuliswa,* remains her most popular script. She works as a traveling saleswoman for a wholesale cornmeal company, selling directly to school administrators, and while she's on her rounds she organizes future productions with the school principals she meets. A number of her own children have played roles in both companies of *Sarafina!* and in *Township Fever,* as have many of her students. Like most of Ngema's young actors, they've built additions to their families' homes, bought a red velvet sofa or two, and sent some brothers and sisters to school.

Ngema asked Zulu to take a leading part in *Township Fever* when the actress who originated the part, Olive Mtsinga, was killed in an automobile accident. *Township Fever* opened at the Majestic Theatre in Brooklyn with Thandi Zulu in the role of Jazz's mother.

▼

After *Woza Albert!,* Percy Mtwa formed a company, Earth Players, and wrote a superb play called *Bopha!,* which opened at the Market Theatre, went to Lincoln Center and the Edinburgh festivals, toured the United States, and has now been adapted into a film, of which Arsenio Hall is the executive producer.

Bheki Mqadi played in *Asinamali!* and in *Township Fever,* married a girl from the original *Sarafina!* company, and has been able to improve his family's life with his earnings. His devotion did pay off, as Ngema promised it would back when he recruited him for *Too Harsh.* Mqadi destroyed his angelic singing voice, however, during the arduous *Asinamali!* tour through America, Australia, Japan, and Europe. In his early thirties now, he speaks in an old man's croak. He is the ranking elder of Committed Artists. Lately he's been living in the house in Bryanston.

Many of Ngema's brothers and sisters have also played roles in his plays. His brother Bhoyi started in *Asinamali!* when he was twenty years old and later played a lead in *Township Fever.* Ngema's youngest brother, Nhlanhla, was in the original company and the movie of *Sarafina!* The financial boon to the Ngema family is compensation for the decline of the land in Hlabisa, which no longer yields a healthy crop. There's little room for grazing anymore, and the herd has dwindled to almost nothing. The family is dependent for their sustenance on Ngema and those brothers and sisters employed by him. The eldest brother, Johannes, has no paying job, but he is the *induna* of *eNhlwathi* now and holds court sessions beneath a tree beside a square house that Zwelikhethabantu built for his family in 1970. The accused sits with his face in the truth-penetrating sun. The elder counselors sit in the shade, listening to testimony and debating the issues of the case. Johannes says little until the end, when he pronounces a judgment based on what he perceives as the majority opinion.

The rondavels are gone. Nhlanhla has just completed construction of a rather elegant ranch-style house. The women still fetch water from the KwaYeni River in drums, which they carry through the countryside on their heads. Visitors bathe in water delivered to them in a dish, using a large bar of lilac-scented soap, reserved for guests. There is no electricity, and for a phone the family must use a party line that serves the entire region. The toilet is a hole in the earth behind the kitchen.

The children eat mostly cornmeal and a little milk, and some suffer from growth-stunting malnutrition or protein-deficiency diseases. There are fewer occasions these days for feasts. But when Ngema is not overseas, longing for his home in Bryanston, he is in Bryanston, pining for Zululand. He is the family hero—catered to and wholly pampered whenever he pays a visit.

He has been making many records lately and has a few movie deals in the works. The *Sarafina!* movie came and went quickly in America, but in South Africa it's an enormous hit. The *Sarafina!* play is still touring here and there. And in Johannesburg, the actors Ngema has already chosen for his next play are training their bodies and minds in his technique. In this play, Ngema wants to invoke the spirit of Muhammad Ali, who has been a hero of the greatest magnitude for South Africans. His brother Bhoyi will play the lead, a Zulu migrant worker who reveres Ali. In some scenes three lives—Ali's, the migrant worker's, and his own—will breathe through Bhoyi at once. It will be a big musical, dominated by the image of Ali, a magnificent man who never conformed to convention, never doubted himself, never backed down from what he believed in. But when the band strikes up, even Ali will have to take his place in the chorus, while a young woman or man steps up to sing the lead and take command of the stage.

EPILOGUE

▼

Shortly after I finished writing this book, Mbongeni Ngema asked me to help him write the new play he was beginning to develop. I immediately accepted the invitation. What follows is my account of the six months during which that play was created—an experience that has surely changed me forever. At the very least, it has made it impossible to write about Mbongeni—or his wife, Leleti Khumalo, or any of the other artists in the company—and refer to them by their formal surnames.

▼

On December 14, 1992, I arrived in Johannesburg to collaborate on the libretto—the "book"—of a musical Mbongeni had already named *Magic at 4 A.M.* Under pressure from the producers to come up with a title so that publicity could begin early, he chose this phrase—a reference to Muhammad Ali's 1974 fight against George Foreman in Zaire, which was broadcast over South African radio at four in the morning—months before a script or a single song was written for the show. Its cost projected at millions of rand. It was to be the first black production ever created for the elegant 1,100-seat Johannesburg Civic Theatre, which for the twenty-five years of its existence had presented touring opera and ballet companies, Christmas pantomimes, and the occasional large-scale musical (most recently *A Chorus Line*) to uniformly white audiences. *Magic at 4 A.M.* was expected to have limited appeal for whites and to draw uninitiated black audiences to the Civic. It was to be a historic occasion in South Africa in an era of historic change.

In 1974, Mbongeni was embarking on his career as a migrant worker. Today he remembers vividly how the Ali-Foreman fight crackled over the air in the predawn hours as he listened along with millions of South Africans—in the townships, in the work hostels, in the gold mines—experiencing, through sound, Ali's eighth-round victory, underscored by the Zairean crowd's cries of *"Ali bomaye! Ali bomaye!"* (Ali kill him!) For Mbongeni and for the legions who regarded Muhammad Ali as a hero, that moment was magical—one of vicarious triumph. This was the thematic point of departure for the play he wanted me to help him write.

In 1974, I had just entered a junior high school in a suburb north of Chicago and had different kinds of things on my mind, although I do remember hearing the news that Ali had beaten Foreman and feeling a small tremble of triumph. I was more of a sports fan than most girls—my father followed all the traditional male American sports with an academic's exhaustive examination and, as I was his only child, conferred some of his fascination on me. Years earlier, I had sided with Ali because he was good-looking and funny, talked in rhymes, and danced around the ring, and I remained loyal. I didn't understand why he had changed his name from Cassius Clay, and was too young to grasp the significance of his refusal to fight in the Vietnam War or the magnitude of his fame, but I wasn't immune to the force of his heroism.

My magical moment with Muhammad Ali came in September 1992, long after he'd retired from boxing. Mbongeni was in New York, publicizing the Disney-distributed film of *Sarafina!* Ali happened to be in town, too, and accepted Mbongeni's invitation to attend the premiere and to discuss the new project, which we then envisioned simplistically as a South African tribute to the champ and for which we hoped to receive his blessing. At dinner before the movie, Ali was quiet, as I gather he almost always is these days. His movements were slow, his eyes seemed vacant, he stumbled slightly when he rose to shake our hands. I had heard people who'd been around him say that they'd found his present, infirm condition sad, even heartbreaking. But I'd never seen him in person before and was staggered by how well he looked when he stood to greet us—younger than his fifty years, strong, tall, broad: he was still beautiful.

Mbongeni talked a little about the play with Ali's "people," who joined us at dinner. Ali himself didn't seem to be absorbing the conversation; the few times he spoke, it was only to request something of the waiter. He did, however, eventually feel the urge to entertain us and after dessert performed a magic trick for our pleasure, one I'm told he does for everyone, making a red handkerchief disappear, reappear, disappear, reappear. . . . Later, at the screening, he seemed deeply moved by *Sarafina!* and suffered visibly during scenes showing acts of cruelty committed by the South African armed forces against black schoolchildren.

The next morning, Mbongeni, his manager, and I met with Ali and two of his representatives in Ali's hotel room, to discuss the new play more formally. Ali sat on the king-size bed that filled most of the room, while we all occupied chairs arranged in a tight semicircle around the bed's lower-right-hand corner. Mbongeni began, painstakingly, to make his presentation to Ali. Shortly into this pitch, however, Ali's breakfast arrived, and he moved far away, to the upper-left-hand corner of the big bed, turning his back to us and seemingly devoting his concentration single-mindedly to his meal.

Now the four men closed up the semicircle and began to talk faster and more freely. Mbongeni spoke, Ali's lawyer asked probing questions, someone else made a suggestion, which was then eagerly developed by another of the men. I had something I wanted to say too, but every time I raised a finger and tried to make my point, someone cut me off before I could get a word out. I was never allowed to proceed beyond the quiet clearing of my throat. These were all very gentle, very gentlemanly men, who surely didn't mean to be rude or bullies. Still, although the act of exclusion was subtle, I saw it clearly: each man who cut me off looked in my eyes as he did it. What was going on was undeniably a minor display of the kind of behavior men continue to be conditioned for in America and in Africa and elsewhere, in spite of their kinder natures.

Then, suddenly, Ali stirred across the room. The conversation halted. He put down his fork and quietly slid his body along the bed. We all turned to him. Ali waved an admonishing finger, like a slow metronome, and with the same smooth, jazzy voice with which he once sang "There'll be a rumble in the jungle," he now commanded in marked rhythm: "Let the lady speak. The lady is trying to speak."

All jaws dropped. Ali's motor control may not be what it used to be, he may not dance much anymore, but he's in there behind those eyes, as aware and focused and heroic as ever. Mbongeni and I turned to each other and smiled. And I forgot what I had wanted to say.

This was the beginning of a long, thrilling, and completely absorbing experience, for which I have only Mbongeni to thank. I'm still not sure why he felt he needed a co-author, but I'm grateful that he did. He made the most generous gift an artist can offer, which is to share his work.

▼

So I went to Johannesburg in December and moved to an apartment on the thirtieth floor of the Mariston Hotel, corner of Claim and Koch, in the Joubert Park area, near Hillbrow, a longtime "gray area" now blacker than gray, almost a township really; a high-crime area in a city that ranks statistically first in the world in far too many violent-crime categories; certainly the most interesting and diverse section of Jo'burg, and my home for the next six months. From my balcony I would watch couples dancing to fifties jazz records at a rooftop New Year's Eve party; I would see a man fall, or be pushed, from his window sometime around Valentine's Day; and one morning in April, just a few days before our opening night, I would awake to the sound of what had become my favorite political anthem, "Umkhonto we Sizwe," sung by a massive division of the longest parade I've ever seen—a passionate, rhythmically throbbing tribute to Chris Hani, the secretary-general of the South African Communist Party, who had been assassinated just a few days earlier.

A woman named Sylvia would come once a week to wash my clothes in the bathtub for less than twenty dollars a month. The meticulous young housekeeper with the sweet smile, who would come every day except Sundays, Christian holidays observed only in Calvinistic countries, and days declared "work stay-aways" by Nelson Mandela, was named, amazingly—it's a highly uncommon name for someone her age—Sarafina.

The residents of the Mariston, an apartment-hotel, included a lot of fortune-seekers and refugees from French-speaking African countries, mostly Zaireans. There were also Eastern Europeans, Chinese, Germans, South Africans, and a couple of Americans in the mix, among the latter group one bitter, solitary, aging theatrical producer who delighted in drinking and swearing and once exclaimed defiantly in the bar, "I'm a sexist and a racist! What do you want from me?" He had been a legitimate producer in New York, Canada, and Ireland in his day and had nothing kind to say about anyone he'd ever worked with. Now all he wanted was to mount productions cheaply in South Africa and make a killing by transporting them home to America, where audiences he seemed to disdain were used to being overcharged.

The entire company of *Magic at 4 A.M.* stayed in the Mariston's efficiency flats. The total number of our group, including company managers, stage managers, sound engineers, and wardrobe mistresses, came to well over fifty, not including lovers, families, and other hangers-on. Mbongeni's brother Siyoni, given the title of Assistant Stage Manager, was charged with driving the minivan that would transport the company to and from the theater every day, in three or four loads.

Like all the apartments in the hotel, mine was decorated completely in olive drab—carpeting, drapery, upholstery, bedding, dinner napkins. It was ugly, but it was clean, private, and simple. On my large dining room table, with its smooth, clear surface, Mbongeni and I would do much of our work. It was a place remote from my home, and I had only one concern there: *Magic at 4 A.M.* I was to write, in legal terms of creative ownership, one half of one third—book, music, and lyrics each accounting for a third of a musical—in four and a half months. Mbongeni, who had many family responsibilities in town and all the complications of being a celebrity in constant demand, had that same amount of time to produce the remaining two and a half thirds, in addition to directing and co-choreographing the production, as well as carrying the full weight of its success or failure upon his shoulders.

Mbongeni and our formidable executive producer, Mannie Manim, had been negotiating with the management and board of directors of the Civic Theatre and with the Johannesburg City Council, which oversees its operations, for many months preceding my involvement. At the beginning of his career, Mannie had worked at the Civic as head of the stage management department, under the general direction of Michal Grobbelaar, who was only just now planning his retirement. Alan Joseph, who had later worked for Mannie at the Market Theatre, had been chosen to replace Grobbelaar, and the transition would begin sometime around our opening night. With the recent defection of much of its key personnel and some mainstay artists, compounded by the effects of a dire national recession, the Market seemed to have been drained of a lot of its nourishing spirit since my last visit. The feeling of unsuppressible vitality, that *this* was the place where everything was happening, where anything could happen and probably would, where all forward-thinking artists inevitably converged—often in spite of a resistance to what some perceived as its bourgeois popularity—was gone. It happens frequently that a place you once idealized falls short of your memory on reexamination, but in this case I was especially sad: I had always felt that if there could be a theater as alive as South Africa's Market, there was hope that such a place might spring up in any of the cruel countries of the world. Now even Mbongeni, whose four principal works had been premiered at the Market, was moving to a new venue.

The Civic's primary business had always been the booking of outside companies into its main theater, not producing original extravaganzas such as Mbongeni envisioned. Among the decisionmakers there was a lot of support and excitement for the project, I'm told, and a feeling that *Magic* would be an appropriate response to the political changes occurring in the country. But an enormous bureaucracy had to evaluate this unorthodox project before approving it; consensus was long in coming, almost long enough to quell the creative impulse, but not quite, not Mbongeni's creative impulse.

When Mbongeni finally received the go-ahead, the only available slot in the Civic's season was a mere five months away. He immediately chose a company from the extended Committed Artists family and from auditions he held in Johannesburg and Durban. Then he had to hurry to Sun City in nearby Bophuthatswana, to serve as a judge in the Miss World Contest, an obligation he'd accepted much earlier. In the meantime, the Crossroads Theatre in New Jersey contributed some funds toward the development of the *Magic* script and paid my way to South Africa. Once I was there, Mannie told me over the phone, the Civic was prepared to take care of me.

When I arrived from New York, Mbongeni was not in the country. From the beauty pageant in Sun City he had traveled to Botswana, where a company of the stage version of *Sarafina!* was performing for the week, seven years after the show's premiere. Many of the Committed Artists chosen to play in *Magic* were in that company. Those who were not and the few new artists Mbongeni had selected from open auditions were already at work in a rehearsal room at the Civic Theatre. They were doing calisthenics, singing scales, and learning dances, which Mbongeni's co-choreographer, Somizi Mhlongo, the twenty-year-old son of Mary Twala and Ndaba Mhlongo, had set temporarily to songs by Paula Abdul and Michael Jackson.

Among the initiates in the company were a few veterans of Gibson Kente's theater—Pinky, Ashanti, Joyce—and three young men with unforgettable names, Remember, Fortune, and Promise, who had been discovered during the Durban auditions. Remember, I would soon learn, spoke very little English but could sing like Marvin Gaye, unerringly, with faultless pitch and a supple range, especially gorgeous in the upper register. Fortune unabashedly told me that he excelled at singing and dancing and also played a number of musical instruments. Promise was in his teens, quieter, and disinclined to boast. It was difficult to discern his specialty or any other aspect of his individuality. In the rehearsal room he would sit demurely, silently, while the others were busy displaying their personalities. Then suddenly he would lift off and do cartwheels across the floor, blurring his telling characteristics.

Mannie Manim was away briefly on holiday. But company manager

Sheila Paris (a longtime associate of Mbongeni's, a Transkeian native who has lived in New York for many years and was flown in for the job) knew that Mbongeni had hired more actors than Mannie's budget could accommodate. When Mbongeni got back, some three or four, at least, would have to go, hearts would have to break. And Sheila, called Mom Sheila by everyone, including me, would have to pick up the pieces. For the time being, however, the company was feeling carefree. They had not only places to stay but highly coveted jobs, the best they could hope for. Everyone was cartwheeling.

A few days later, when Mbongeni arrived from Botswana, he and I began immediately to sketch out a structure for the play. The first couple of nights, we did this brainstorming at a shebeen in the apartment of a longtime friend to Mbongeni and all the Committed Artists—a man famous around Jo'burg, well known as someone not to cross and a very good person to have on your side in such a tough town. Going to his shebeen is just like paying a drinking visit to a friend—until it's time to leave, when even a close friend must pay his tab.

We got there very late at night and sat in the living room till just before sunrise. Mom Sheila came, too, and kept our host company while Mbongeni and I focused on the play. We knew that our hero would be a worker and amateur boxer living in a war-torn, single-sex hostel. His very life would be a homage to Muhammad Ali, his idol, whose example would keep him from willingly partaking in wars he doesn't believe in. At the moment, the hostels were hotbeds for violent clashes between followers of the ANC and Inkatha, at which white men in balaclava masks and black makeup, the infamous "third force," were often sighted, presumably instigating the conflict. We chose against setting our hostel in Soweto or any other major township and decided to place it in a workers' compound at a fictitious gold mine on the outskirts. Mbongeni wanted to radiate the positive virtues Ali has promoted throughout his life—peace, heroism, cultural unity, spiritual devotion, and respect for one's ancestry—onto South African characters warring today in opposition to these principles. But he didn't want simply to reflect images in the newspaper or pick sides in the real-life conflict. Life in the hostels is isolated, cramped, dark, dangerous. A gold mine bored miles into the earth seemed to be a good metaphor for this life: profoundly isolated, darker than night, the work incalculably treacherous. And Mbongeni's imagination was excited by the scenic potential.

The boxing imagery would play heavily, too, and I relished it. I had always seen boxing as an ironic vehicle for someone headed toward outspoken pacifism; punching, pummeling, demeaning an antagonist, calling him a gorilla, was a funny way for Ali, a proud black man, to show respect for a brother. Ali's eloquence, trash talking, moral integrity, self-love, god-love, ring dancing, rope-a-doping, his monumental proportions, his grace, his physical fierceness, his beauty: how could one man embody so many opposing qualities? Well, just like the world—and South Africa—can. And the degree to which a man can keep all his temperaments in balance appears to be the degree to which he's at peace. Ali seemed the perfect icon to loom over a play set in a country that so badly needs peace and is so far from achieving the necessary equilibrium.

The story elements were a little disjointed and confusing at this point, but we had fun sorting them out and pulling them together during our first month of work together. Mbongeni would frequently clasp my wrist, or I his, in a paroxysm of discovery. We often laughed till tears rolled out of our eyes. I'd never had such an effortless rapport with anyone. Of course, it helped that I'd researched his life and could easily locate his points of reference. This was to be Mbongeni's work, and it would be in many ways specific to him. It would come largely out of his experience and only in subtextual ways out of mine. We were in sync. He has a huge patriarchal ego that dominates his personal life, but in our work together he was open-minded, accepted suggestions and revisions effortlessly, and absolutely shared the play with me. When he found my work especially good, he never hesitated to say so, emphatically. When he didn't like it, he suggested a constructive alternative rather than take the risk of hurting my feelings with criticism. We were an odd pair with almost nothing in common in our personal backgrounds, but it truly worked.

The first adjective I would use to describe Mbongeni is "fearless." He works without any concern for failure, presuming only success. "This is going to be *better* than *Sarafina!*" he'd say to the press when they wondered, cynically, if he could live up to his past triumph. He is motivated by an enthusiasm for his ideas—a voice so loud in his head that if he had any self-doubts he surely wouldn't be able to hear them—and follows every impulse unhesitatingly. In our work, he was drawn to big, emotional climaxes with a high risk of sentimentality, which I tended to cower away from. He hired actors he liked and worried later about how he would cast them.

He had retained Leleti to be one of the stars in the play; she had never played any part except Sarafina but had grown magnificently with the role and, with the film's successful release in South Africa, had become a beloved national superstar, appearing regularly on the covers of magazines. She would be a certain box-office draw. He had also hired Seipati Sothoane, the young woman who played Sarafina in the second company of the play. Mbongeni had always wanted these two actresses to work together. They bore not even the slightest physical resemblance, but they performed with a similar mesmerizing intensity. One night, he gripped my wrist and said, "They should be sixteen-year-olds! They should be twins!" Although the problem of finding starring roles for two physically unmatched twin girls in the all-male scenario we'd developed flabbergasted me at first, Mbongeni never even blinked at the challenge.

As usual in Mbongeni's work, the basis for this play was the company. The "magic at 4 A.M.," the Ali-Foreman fight that had been Mbongeni's starting point, moved to a subordinate position in our imagery. The story changed every time Mbongeni promoted a bit player to a supporting role. Very early on, he had chosen his brother Bhoyi to play the lead. Bhoyi, who had been training in a boxing gym for weeks before I arrived in Johannesburg, came to me frequently during that first month, begging for hints about his character, concerned that the job would be too big for him. But Bhoyi needn't have worried; his part was built to fit him, to be filled by him, as all the roles were designed to illuminate unique characteristics of the actors who played them. (The music worked much the same way. Mbongeni hired all his favorite musicians—including his old friend Skhumbuzo, the guitarist—and as he wrote songs was often inspired by what he knew they could do with them.) The remaining members of the cast would be featured as dancers or singers, according to their strengths. Remember, for example, would sing many r&b solos that Mbongeni wrote especially for him.

Before we really had a handle on the story, Mbongeni and I presented its elements to Sarah Roberts, the set and costume designer, and Mannie, doubling as lighting designer, who were anxious—almost frantic, actually—to get things under way in the theater. The antithesis of the "poor theater" of Mbongeni's origins, the Civic posed many dizzying options and obstacles. Because the main stage was built to accommodate operas and to store mammoth sets, it is cavernously deep, expansively broad in the wings, and has the capacity to fly many massive sets in from the ceiling. The orchestra pit sinks, a number of elevators allow the levitating of actors or sets, and the stage has the capability to revolve. The Civic was not designed for Mbongeni's kind of theater, which emphasizes the actor over the scenery. And since acoustically it was deficient for our purposes, better suited for operatic voices and classical orchestras than for an electrically amplified band and singers, it would need some improvement in that area.

Mannie and Sarah had worked with Mbongeni since his earliest days at the Market. Knowing that the play would long be in an unfinished state of metamorphosis, even beyond the opening night, and that Mbongeni would never be satisfied, they had an impressive laissez-faire attitude about the future. Sarah, with only sketchy, convoluted information from us, began to design her set. Soon we refined our outline, but by then she'd already built an elaborate model with pieces that could be endlessly modified to adapt to the play's inevitable transformations.

To learn something about a gold mine, Mbongeni and I, Bhoyi, and a few others from the company went in search of one on the West Rand, an hour or so outside Johannesburg. Someone in our group knew of a mine in this area that encompassed a hostel named Ezulweni (Heaven, in Zulu), which Mbongeni liked the sound of. We found the place—a two-shaft operation owned by one of the major mining interests—a good distance from the highway. Affixed to trees on either side of the long private approach road were colorful signs printed with enigmatic phrases, in English and Afrikaans: "Glass Eyes Cannot

See!" "A Wooden Leg Cannot Support a Family!" "The Workers at This Mine Are the Best and the Safest in the World!" Were these messages intended for prospective workers, to admonish or entice? Considering that most work-seekers would be functionally illiterate, few of them speaking English or Afrikaans, probably not. Were the signs for visitors, to give the impression—perhaps true—that safety is a high priority to a management always looking for ways to impress on their employees the consequences of recklessness?

The ten thousand men who worked here lived behind a gate in a hostel, which sat quarantined behind another gate; they were free to come and go, we'd soon learn, but most would have little time or energy to travel the road to the outside world. On Sundays they might visit a friend in the small township nearby, on Christmas make long journeys to their families in the rural areas of South Africa, Lesotho, and Mozambique. A billboard at the gate provided questionable statistics related to the rate of injury and fatality per shift. And four stars on another sign were supposed to signify something else about safety, something cryptic, which we didn't understand. We would soon be told that industry regulations require the management to post this last bit of information for prospective employees, to let them know what kind of risk they're taking in working here.

After a lengthy conversation at the front gate with a young black guard, who recognized Mbongeni and seemed thrilled to meet him, we were finally allowed in and directed through the compound to the Heaven we sought. We passed through two more gates—past office blocks, past the west shaft—before we arrived at a prisonlike wall marked EZULWENI, through which men were freely coming and going past guards positioned at turnstiles. Being female, I was not allowed to enter the hostel area this first time and had to wait in the car while the men popped in briefly. On subsequent visits, with permission from the head office, we were taken on extensive tours. We spent hours one day with the manager of the west shaft, who explained the workings of the mine. We toured the hostel (there was another one next door, called Emafini—Clouds) and found a vast complex of two-story dormitories and much more, an entire world, lacking only women. There were places to eat, drink beer, play pinball, a stadium for soccer and boxing, a bank for saving money, a shop for spending it, a public-address system broadcasting music and sports events, and a great deal of intramural comradeship. The hostel's manager, a white man, explained that the workers like to segregate themselves ethnically; he showed us the Shangaan section, which was pristine. "Go in. They don't mind. They'll be proud," he said, and urged us into one of the rooms without asking the residents for permission. Four bunk beds were tightly made as if for military inspection. Combs, Bibles, books, boxes of sugar, bottles of deodorant were displayed in geometric arrangements. Hanging on the wall, like objets d'art, were two new women's dresses. Our guide smiled. "For his wife, you see! He bought them here at the shop. Oh, our men are very happy here." But there was something sad about the formless dresses, made of strident fabrics, chosen with pride by a man from a limited selection in a compound shop stocked by other men.

Mbongeni wandered to the Zulu section, against the apparent wishes of the manager. Here the men were laughing and swearing obstreperously. Shirts and pants hung drying from windows and over the railing on the second story. Bits of mildly vulgar flattery—translated later—were tossed playfully at Sarah, who joined us on this particular day, and at me. The Shangaan section had been like foreign territory to Mbongeni and the other men in our group; they tiptoed through it like embarrassed tourists, just as I did. Stumbling into the Zulu section, they instantly relaxed and laughed with the men, reacting with the kind of relief I might have felt had we encountered a dorm filled with Midwesterners.

We came back another day to attend a marathon inter-mine boxing tournament, remarkable for the fierceness and brutality of the fights. And on another visit we descended about a mile and a half into the earth.

For our underground tour we were fully equipped—T-shirt, white coveralls, socks, gum boots, helmet, black vinyl overcoat, gloves, a belt with the heavy battery pack necessary for the light on the helmet, and a cumbersome emergency oxygen pack. The mine overseer's demonstration of how to use the oxygen was unlike that on an airplane: "In the unlikely event . . .," to which no one pays attention. When this man said, "I hope nothing happens, but if it does, this is what you do," we made him repeat the demonstration three times before we stepped onto the first of several elevators that would take us down.

These elevators come in various sizes, with maximum occupancy posted as 10, 20, or 65. They travel a good deal faster and farther than your typical office-building elevator, swaying madly as water sprays in. Many men commute some forty-five minutes vertically to work every morning and don't make the return trip or stop for a meal until the end of their shift, eight hours later, longer if they work overtime, as many do. Disembarking, we trekked through wide tunnels and narrow ones, sliding down, clambering up, gripping the rock surface, stumbling down crude ladders, sloshing through mud, skirting men wielding power drills. The deeper we went, the hotter it became. We shed our jackets. The explosives used daily to blast new stopes into the rock wall had left a powerful, dizzying smell of ammonia. We were told that it takes two tons of the low-grade rock excavated here to produce two grams of gold. We were not taken to the place of really brutal work, deeper in the earth, where black men slither on their stomachs through seemingly impossible spaces to get at every tiny speck.

The workers we saw wore plastic whistles on strings around their necks, for use in case of emergency. They also carried the heavy oxygen packs and were supposed to know the fastest route to the nearest Emergency Refuge Room, which was supplied with food, water, and air, and could be lifesaving if they happened to be nearby when a "bump" (an earth tremor) began to shake things up.

After resurfacing filthily a few hours later, we showered and changed in a disinfectant-reeking locker room, then were treated to Cokes in the management tavern. On the way there, Mbongeni and the guys encountered some black workers, who told them that accidents happen regularly underground; at that moment, several men had been trapped in rock for days. It was their opinion that this was a distinctly dangerous mine. Do not believe what you read, they said. The elevators, for instance, the smallest of which I had found stiflingly overcrowded with just the seven of us, usually carry twice as many black workers as the legal maximum occupancy printed on prominent signs.

The visits to the mine were critical to the development of our story, and immediately afterward we plotted out the entire play, scene by scene. But even earlier, as soon as he began to get a sense of the core of the work, Mbongeni had determined which of the actors he would not find indispensable roles for and would have to release because of budgetary constraints. Only a week or so after he returned from Botswana, he delivered the news, with great difficulty (when it comes to such tasks, Mbongeni is not fearless), to the four unfortunates: two young women, whose names I had never learned, and Fortune and Promise.

I ran into the two men in the hotel that morning. Fortune, the more forthright of the pair, said to me urgently: "Mr. Mbongeni Ngema refuses to accept us in his play!" He examined me carefully, checking me for signs of influence, and then pressed me anyway: "Lady, I think you can tell him he must accept us. I can play my penny whistle, and I am singing and dancing and playing my saxophone." It had to be true that Fortune was gifted. No one without talent could promote himself so assuredly. Promise, by contrast, was paralyzed, with bright-red, thunderstruck eyes. Knowing I could do nothing for them, I tried to be sympathetic. I told them that they'd chosen a terrible career, that I have actor friends in New York who get rejected three times a day, but I saw instantly that this comparison could be no comfort to Fortune and Promise. They would probably have to wait until Mbongeni announced auditions for his next play before they would have a shot at jobs anywhere near as good as the ones they'd just so irreversibly lost.

Fortune possessed the practical ability to walk away from pain and stayed at the hotel that day, bravely preparing to return home to Durban. But Promise was drawn to the scene of his anguish. He went to rehearsal, where, sobbing, he watched the company dance the dances he would never dance again. Members of the company tried to console him, but they found it impossible and returned to their work. Later, Promise found refuge in the production office, where he sat curled up in a ball at Mom Sheila's feet, quietly whimpering while she tenderly patted his back.

▼

While at night we developed the story, by day Mbongeni wrote music, nearly thirty songs in as many days—songs typically related thematically to the play but not necessarily to the characters or the specific events we were exploring. The ideas we discussed during our meetings might lead him to a lyric or to a fully orchestrated, fully choreographed number, which as yet only he could see and hear. A melody might come to him in his car on the way to the theater from Bryanston. Regardless of the extent of his preparation, when he arrived at work he'd go immediately to the electric keyboard and gather the company around—stars, chorus, dancers, everyone. There were surely hundreds, maybe thousands, of portable chairs in the Civic complex, but for some reason there were never enough in the rehearsal room, where most seats had to accommodate at least two bodies; three or four chairs could form a kind of bench for seven or eight. "Comportment!" Mbongeni would command, strictly, like a schoolmaster. The class would obediently hush, straighten themselves, and turn their unwavering concentration to him while he worked out a chord progression or jotted down a few lyrics on a pad of paper. Then he would look up and begin to teach.

If the composition called for a solo or a number of solos, he'd work with those artists first, while the rest of the company wrote the notes (do-re-me) and lyrics in their personal steno books, just in case one of the soloists didn't work out and Mbongeni needed a replacement. Then he would simultaneously compose, arrange, and teach the backing vocals to the chorus, using voices like keys on a piano to create rich harmonics and emotional dynamics. Next, the musical director, Eddie Mathibe, having heard the song maybe once or twice, would take command of the keyboard while Mbongeni refined the whole. He wrote in many styles—gospel-influenced, Zulu traditional, r & b, *mbaqanga*—never suffered from writer's block, never got stuck in a rut of redundancy, and quickly produced some of his best music to date. In my opinion, this was the finest group of singers Mbongeni had ever assembled. Some of the voices—Remember, David, Futhi, Sonto, Sibusiso, Velephi, Thandi—were almost too sublime to be true. I attended nearly every one of these sessions, occasionally helping Mbongeni find a word for a lyric but mostly just snapping my fingers, swaying in the corner. I would have days when I would feel lost in Africa, dislocated, or lonely . . . until I looked at the faces and heard the voices.

At the end of the first month, Mbongeni and I stood together in front of the piano and presented our complete scenario to the company, while they stared up at us. Very well comported they were and gratifyingly attentive, laughing at the right moments, clucking their tongues and crying out when we described some scene of woe or abomination. At the end, they applauded.

In the phase of work that followed, Mbongeni and I wrote disconnected scenes. With our outline as a guide, we began with the last scene and proceeded in no particular order, according only to Mbongeni's whim. I would print out the pages on my computer at the hotel. Together, we would read them aloud to the company, then we'd give stapled copies to the actors involved in the scene, who would accompany me to a room where I would help them with their lines. In the meantime, Mbongeni would work on other things.

Mbongeni and I wrote most of the scenes together from scratch, improvising the dialogue in my apartment in a comfortable give-and-take. He was tireless. One day, we wrote four major scenes in rapid sequence. "Let's do another," Mbongeni would say. All of me would cry, "No, not another—I *can't*," but I'd comply in spite of myself and soon see that it could indeed be done. Sometimes he would arrive with a scene already alive in his head; I would transcribe it into the computer, and together we would add and edit. Often, after discussing what should happen in a particular scene, Mbongeni would leave it to me to draft on my own while he addressed himself to some other aspect of the play. When I was finished, he'd come over, and I would read it aloud to him. Then we'd pare it down and change it.

The real revision came later, in rehearsal—and painfully. We wrote a few storytelling scenes, which were quite long, far too long. Through rehearsals and more rehearsals, as the actors learned and relearned their lines and their blocking, we shed paragraph after paragraph. Mbongeni, who in these moments could be quite unemotional and businesslike, would turn to me and say, "We don't need this." It was sometimes difficult to take, but he was always right, and I soon began to enjoy the process. After the work of putting everything that interested us into the script, the pleasure now came from lightening the load, discovering how much we could live happily without. The discarded stories had not been a waste of time; absorbed now by the actors, they'd given them a lasting sense of the depth of their characters' history and motivations, which would enrich the performances.

By the time Mbongeni found fitting places for most of his songs and we began running sequentially through the first and then the second act, our rehearsals for several weeks had been going usually sixteen hours straight, with breaks only for meals, catered on the premises by our enterprising friend from the shebeen. We rarely went home before three in the morning. Our schedule for one week in February was: Monday, 10:00 A.M.–2:00 A.M.; Tuesday, 12:00 noon–4:00 A.M.; Wednesday, 2:00 P.M.–6:00 A.M.; Thursday, 5:00 P.M.–1:00 A.M.; Friday, 1:00 P.M.–4:00 A.M.; Saturday, amazingly, a day off; Sunday, as usual, off. Mbongeni claimed that the middle of the night is the time of his freest creativity. But it became clear to me that one of the most compelling benefits of the job for him is the control he has over so many lives. On Friday of the week outlined above, he announced fiendishly at midnight, to forty people ranging in age from eighteen to fifty, "We're going to work until dawn!" and listened impassively to the groans and moans of the company. Then at quitting time, he said with a good-natured smile, "The next call is"—and then paused for dramatic effect—"10:00 A.M. . . . ," and then allowed another gap for company groans before finally saying, "the day after tomorrow!" whereupon he watched gleefully as the actors cheered, squealed, and cartwheeled. "Thank you, Bhuti Mbongeni! Thank you!"

Mbongeni seemed to take an even greater pleasure in the work itself and usually guided the actors lovingly through their scenes. But when all else failed, his directorial style was authoritarian. Most of the actors were in their early twenties and had worked for Mbongeni for the entirety of their careers. Some were older and had known him during his humble beginnings. Others were related to him by blood, one by marriage. No matter how comfortable they were with Mbongeni on a personal level, all of the actors and most of the musicians, some of whom were older than he, tended, at work, to deify him to the point of trepidation. He reinforced his position by unpredictably slipping into the schoolmaster mode and, until the newly formed actors' union asked him to stop, disciplining off-pitch singers with a wooden cane smacked smartly on the palms of their outstretched, yielding hands, a common form of punishment in South African schools, one Mbongeni himself had received many times. When an actor would fudge a bit of business, or a musician miss a cue by a beat, Mbongeni would usually stop the rehearsal in its tracks and instruct the company to return to the beginning of the scene, the act, or whatever stretch of material we were working on, much as a drill sergeant will punish an individual private by ordering the rest of the company to do push-ups.

On February 22, I wrote a letter to a friend: "Since December 20 an entire story has been dreamed up, a script written, a set designed, more than 25 songs composed and, now, orchestrated (an 11-piece band has joined us in the rehearsal room), and a few of the numbers have been choreographed, although Mbongeni is saving that job for last." It had been an absolutely absorbing period of time, during which we all gave ourselves over completely to Mbongeni's will, caprice, and vision and tried very hard to adjust our inner fine tunings in order to feel creative when he did, in the hours just before the sun rose.

On April 1, the day we moved rehearsals into the theater proper, the previous day's work ended at 6:45 A.M. I decided to walk home for my day's sleep, a good twenty-to-thirty-minute walk. The sky was clear and my senses wide open. For the first time since the beginning of my stay in Johannesburg, I was awake to the foreignness of my surroundings. I heard every funny high-pitched car squeak. Big, boxy, empty buses screeched strangely. In some places, the sidewalk had been dug up to repair subterranean workings, revealing earth that was a deep, deep, mineral red. A little black girl, about five years old, held her brother, about three, by the hand and led him unchaperoned across a busy street toward some apparently regular daily destination. A group of gigantic Afrikaner women, with red hair and unevenly toned skin, barreled down on me, arguing inscrutably among themselves. The dawning that I was in a foreign place, as far away as the southernmost tip of Africa, had been induced, finally, by the sounds and came as a kind of relief: I had momentarily relocated my point of reference.

When I got home I stripped one of my two single beds and stuffed the sheets and all my towels in a pillowcase, which I placed outside the door for Sarafina. (The linens and towels were washed each Thursday;

if I didn't put them out, she would come in an hour and pound on my door until I let her in.) I shoved a slab of buttered bread down my throat so that I wouldn't wake from hunger. At 8:00 A.M., I went to sleep, waking again at 1:00 P.M. to return to the theater.

▼

On the days preceding opening night, seven previews had been scheduled. During that week, several crises befell us as a company, presented here in no particular order of chronology, gravity, or sorrow:

The day before our first public performance, one of my favorite actresses, Futhi, who played a major supporting role and sang a number of solos, and for whom no understudy had been chosen, was hospitalized for a problem that would keep her out of the show until opening night.

The three-year-old son of Ashanti (a fine performer with an indomitably wry sense of humor) died of dehydration resulting from a severe case of diarrhea.

During the last preview, Bhoyi, the star of the show, went temporarily blind when the styling spray in his hair dripped into his eyes and triggered a severe allergic reaction. (He recovered just in time for the opening.)

A lead vocalist was beaten up by another company member—her boyfriend—hospitalized, and forced to stay out of the show for two weeks.

On the tenth of April, two days before our first preview, Chris Hani was murdered. This was less of a direct tragedy for us, of course, than it was for everyone in South Africa and for the Hani family. We canceled two of our seven previews in observance of nationally declared work stay-aways.

Ashanti, who had followed her doctor's instructions faithfully and still couldn't save her child, was unspeakably distraught when her baby died. Mom Sheila went to her, comforted her, and cleaned the child's body before he was taken away to the morgue. The next day, Sheila took up a collection among the company and helped to arrange the funeral.

In New York, I had known Mom Sheila primarily as a hostess with that extraordinary South African gift for accommodating an unlimited number of guests in a severely limited space. Sitting in the neat living room of her two-bedroom Harlem apartment for an intimate chitchat, I would wait to see how many South African expatriates would emerge from the bedroom wing to say hello. All these people would be staying with her, some of them for months, a year, perhaps longer. When the company of *Sarafina!* or *Township Fever* was in town, Mom Sheila would throw almost nightly parties, packed, hilarious affairs, with sometimes heavy drinking, dancing and speechmaking, and, from time to time, prayer.

She had toured all over the world as manager of the second company of *Sarafina!,* but I had never seen her at work until our collaboration on *Magic at 4 A.M.* Aside from dispensing the payroll and coordinating press interviews and executing other managerial tasks, Sheila was responsible for mending broken hearts and mediating personal disputes, however trivial or intimate. When an actor was brutally assaulted on the streets of Hillbrow, Sheila was summoned to gather him up at the police station. A cast member would need to borrow money to buy his children food or to pay off a loan shark, and he would call Sheila first. If at 4:00 A.M. there was too much noise coming from the twenty-second floor, where many of the cast members stayed, the Mariston management would call Sheila. Her phone rang at all hours. And when there was a death in the company, she would make the necessary arrangements.

The first funeral Sheila organized was for thirty-five-year-old Skhumbuzo Mabaso, Mbongeni's guitarist friend from the aluminum factory, who died in the hospital from a chronic internal ailment. Skhumbuzo was beloved by Mbongeni and by all the Committed Artists who had worked with him over the years. He was a kind, gentle man and a brilliant musician. His service, largely subsidized by Mbongeni, was held on February 13 in Vosloorus, a township south of Johannesburg.

The first phase took place in a newly constructed shopping center at the threshold of the township. Here friends offered testimonials and tributes, the *Magic* company performed a few songs, and the mourners periodically broke out into anguishing, moaning dirges, as latecomers straggled in.

By the time the cortege arrived at the graveyard, deeper in the heart of the township, an enormous crowd had assembled. Funerals are the biggest social events in South Africa. ("Were you at Sipho's funeral?" I heard someone ask a friend. "Oh, yes, it was beautiful. But Jabu's was the biggest one this year. Everyone I've ever met was there.") The parking area reminded me of the outdoor rock concerts I went to when I was in high school and how hard it was to find a place to park; after the show it was even harder to locate your car, acres away from the main event.

Mbongeni and the *Magic* company encircled Skhumbuzo's coffin and sang, leaving me on my own, far away in the crowd. If I craned my neck, I could see that someone had placed a guitar on Skhumbuzo's coffin. But I had a more satisfying view of the people and pageantry on the outskirts of our group. From time to time, mourners attending concurrent burials in adjacent plots noticed Mbongeni and Leleti and pointed or leaped up, crying, "Sarafina!"

One of the nearby services was a Methodist affair. As I remember it now, the preachers stood beneath a canopy in big black robes accented by collars of red or blue. They wore big hats and carried scepters, which they twirled, dancing. One preacher held a stick garlanded with resonant bells, which jingled as he hopped from foot to foot. The ranking preacher was round and jolly, like Santa Claus. His flock bounced up and down with him, singing merrily. The deceased must have lived a long life that entitled him to a lively tribute. The folk in the crowd, most of them adult, many elderly, seemed to be in a mirthful trance. The look in their eyes was of fresh liberation.

On the other side of Skhumbuzo's plot was a funeral for a young gangster—a *tsotsi*. Heavy, dark, intoxicated with grief, it was underscored by haunting dirges. When the coffin was lowered into the earth, a young man fired several shots spontaneously into the air, inspiring a number of others in the congregation to reach for their guns and do the same.

All three enormous flocks merged and blended at the borders.

Afterward, we trekked to our cars and drove to Skhumbuzo's home, where we ate and drank and sang some more. Skhumbuzo's widow, who had had a hard time keeping her legs beneath her all day, sat silently now, bundled in blankets. One of his children attached herself to Mom Sheila's side.

That night, not wanting to miss out on an opportunity for surreal South African contrast, Sheila and I went to the gala opening performance of the regional ballet company's presentation of *The Merry Widow*, which preceded *Magic* in the Civic's production schedule. The ornate painted sets and the frilled and bejeweled costumes were delectable, like wedding cakes and petits fours. In the audience we were surrounded by white people in tuxedos and evening gowns. Before the third act, ushers passed out neat little bundles of carnations, which we hurled onto the stage during curtain calls, aiming for the merry widow.

▼

Peter Brook wrote (and Mbongeni took hope) that he could "take any empty space and call it a bare stage. A man walks across this empty space whilst someone else is watching him, and this is all that is needed for an act of theater to be engaged." At the Civic Theatre on April 21, opening night of *Magic at 4 A.M.,* the arriving audience certainly didn't need to see an actor to know that something dramatic was about to take place. Their walk through the stately Civic Centre, past the fountains and the public sculptures, up to the illuminated front doors, would tell them so, as would the gilded, chandeliered, red-carpeted lobby inside. The bronze busts of former Johannesburg mayors and dead arts patrons, at stern attention in the foyer, would signify the pageantry if not the breathing life of the theater. Someone seeking sacredness in the rite might find it tainted by the presence of so many armed guards—always in surplus at the Civic—but might be so inured to guns, being after all a South African, that he wouldn't even notice them among the swirl of gowns, tuxedos, and—yes—dazzling African robes and dashikis.

Shortly before eight o'clock, life bigger than life would blow into the theater when Muhammad Ali arrived with his entourage. Having some months earlier given us his official blessing by fax, he would now present it in person. He would take his seat in the "Mayor's Box," the place of honor at the rear of the orchestra (paradoxically one of the worst seats in the house because of its position under the lip of the balcony, which distorts the sound). Then at last, when all 1,100 people settled down, a man—two, actually—would walk into the empty space of the stage and look out.

Throughout most of the play, a striking silhouette of the shaft and connected workings of a gold mine stood suggestively upstage, behind the onstage band. Occasionally a mesh fence would come down in front of it to indicate the compound; sometimes the mine piece would fly up whole to the ceiling to be replaced by a silhouette of a church, or of a row of plain township houses. For the first scene only, which presented miners at work through mime and dance, a set simulating rock and darkness filled most of the stage. The lights were stunning and evocative, but there were few embellishing effects until the finale, which held a few visual surprises, and most of the action was performed on a bare stage. The performances, music, dances, and direction had such essential dramatic force that even though the story line is more conventionally linear than most of Mbongeni's texts, it's almost impossible for me to give a satisfying breakdown of *Magic*. But I'll attempt a summary:

A young man named Shisa Boy (a mine term for the one who handles the explosives, literally "fire boy"; played by Dumisani Dlamini) has been sent to Ezulweni mine by a bad white cop named Skiet to overthrow Ezulweni's champion boxer, Shaka Zulu (Bhoyi Ngema). Shaka calls himself Muhammad Ali and knows every detail of the champ's career; he fights like him, talks like him, and rankles the establishment like him. Skiet, existing only offstage, wants him beaten. Shisa assures his white boss:

Even if he had six hands, I'd fuck him up for you. And I hear that he talks too much. Don't worry. I'll shut up his big mouth. I'll break his jaw just like Ken Norton broke Ali's jaw. When I'm through with him he's never going to talk again. He'll behave himself. He'll be a sweet boy. And he'll listen.

Even though he has badly injured his hand in a mining accident. Shaka unhesitatingly accepts Shisa's challenge to box. He summons his best friend, Idi Amin (Bheki Mqadi), and together they chant their credo:

Fight like a Zulu warrior!
Dance like a Zulu girl!
Rumble, Shaka Zulu, rumble!

We change scenes and go to a church in the township adjacent to Ezulweni, where we meet two orphaned twin girls named Sweetie (Leleti Khumalo) and Sweetheart (Seipati Sothoane), who tell us their story: They came with their mother to the Johannesburg area from Zululand eleven years ago, when they were five. Although their father had spinelessly abandoned them on the day they were born, their mother seemed still to love him and, believing him to be in Johannesburg, undertook this fateful journey, in the course of which she was killed, an event, the twins tell us, they don't like to talk about. They were discovered by a sanctimonious preacher (David Manqele), who brought them to this church, his home. He also works as the preacher at Ezulweni, around which the lives of all the residents of this township revolve. In the preacher's home they are merely two Cinderellas, allowed no pleasure, only work, and, worst of all, forced to put up with the preacher's real daughter, the spoiled and selfish Lunga (Futhi Mhlongo).

From the church the preacher's family goes to the boxing exhibition at the mine, where the entire ensemble occupies bleachers and, before the fight begins, sings a song titled "African Solution."

From this point on, the play develops around the rivalry between Shaka Zulu and Shisa Boy as it spirals, enveloping the other men in the hostel and dividing them into enemy camps. Simultaneously, the lives of the two foes become entwined with the tales of the twins and Lunga—serendipitously, comically, romantically, at first, and then, in the second act, tragically. My vested interest in allowing the play to speak for itself in performance prevents me from giving away the details of the integrating events (except to say that Shaka charms the girls by performing a magic trick with a red handkerchief). But it probably won't come as a surprise to learn that a violent death does in the end occur.

I won't ever forget the first time this death scene was rehearsed. In the public performances, real assault rifles—disabled, of course—were used. In rehearsal, however, we didn't have such aids to the imagination. The murderers shot their victim with invisible machine guns, ludicrously misaimed. Then, in an act of gratuitous cruelty (predestined by Mbongeni), another man onstage impaled the poor victim with a push broom standing in for a pitchfork. As unconvincing as this demonstration was, when the rest of the company entered the scene to mourn the death communally, they were all, without exception, devastated and weeping. No actor in my experience has ever been readier to believe a make-believe death scene—one performed in an absolutely empty space, with neither props, fake blood, nor atmospheric lighting—than a South African. For hours afterward, some of the actors could not be consoled and continued to sob, thinking undoubtedly of someone who had died in a similar way, someone they'd loved.

▼

On opening night, the play ran an epic three and a half hours, a good deal shorter than it had been in the rehearsal room, but still too long: a fault underlined in every review I read—most positive, some mixed, a few spiteful. In the following weeks, we continued to work on the play, and we cut a half hour out of it—most of it from the musical finale—before the scheduled closing night in July. (Before the play begins to tour outside South Africa, it will certainly change again.)

At a certain point—somewhere around the first of April, when the pressure was intense—I had become less an equal partner to Mbongeni than a persistent voice in his head, sometimes nagging, sometimes encouraging. Later, after opening night, we would often watch the show together, both taking notes. He was especially fussy about the sound mix and, because he didn't want to miss a chord, would send me on frequent trips to deliver urgent instructions to the engineer. In postmortem sessions with the company, having mastered Mbongeni's natural speech patterns and rhythms, I could seamlessly slip my comments in between his. I had learned since December that to be a Committed Artist is to be committed, first of all, to Mbongeni.

There were some days, early on, when I felt let down in my expectations of what it was to be a Committed Artist. In rehearsal, I watched incredulously as trivial disputes, questions, and complaints—usually related not to the work itself but to the food in rehearsal or program billing or hotel room inequities—exploded into monumental turmoil, necessitating marathon company meetings. The most serious arguments resulted in tears and ill-considered insults. The most unforgivable demonstrations of disrespect were usually returned with violent threats: "I'll fuck you up," a man might say—though never a woman, as swearing was tolerated only as a male privilege—or, more commonly, *"Ngizokushaya"* ("I'm going to hit you," in Zulu). Gossip and jealousy were common diversions from work. Reflecting a societal tolerance for such behavior, some of the men regularly used their fists to resolve romantic disputes. A number of company members, following another lamentable trend in South Africa, drank far, far too much on days off—binges during which they lost themselves completely, obliterating all their beautiful qualities. I had imagined that the work would always supersede other concerns, routines, and furies, and, naively, that the exigencies of South African life would never be allowed to intrude. Today that's impossible to imagine, and what's amazing to me now is that in spite of the constant interference of real-life unrest, the work flourished as it did.

One day during his early struggles with self-confidence, Bhoyi came to me and said, trying to cheer us both, "We're going to be a big success, don't worry. If we work hard, we'll make a lot of money. We'll be rich, I promise you." I suppose what I had expected was that Bhoyi might come to me and say: "If we work really hard we'll touch people's souls, change the world, and incarnate the spirits of our ancestors." This was South Africa, after all, not Broadway. But the fact was that for Bhoyi and the rest of the company, the sense of soulfulness, of exorcising pain, was so intrinsic to the work—was the definition of the work—that it never would have occurred to them to discuss it or be self-conscious about it. Bhoyi had struggled plenty in his life—he had worked as a coal miner, and he told me one day that he had enjoyed the job compared to others he'd had, relishing especially the brotherhood that had existed among the men. After his brother Mbongeni trained him to act, he had leading roles in *Asinamali!* and *Township Fever,* but he hadn't worked since the very beginning of 1991. He was in love now and wanted to marry and needed money to pay *lobola.* Everyone in the company needed money badly for their families and for themselves. They would have to wait a little longer for a universally elected government and longer still for peace, and they could; they did not want to wait, as Fortune and Promise and so many other South Africans would have to, to support their families.

At the moment, nobody in South Africa has a better knack for commercial theater than Mbongeni, and nobody enjoys success of this kind more than he. He has shown that what one must do to be successful in this field is to produce the very finest work possible. And the work is telling the stories of one's people and beloved ancestors, using every feeling, ability, experience, and technique one has available to the fullest extent possible. It's an absolutely wonderful job, and not everyone can do it.

In the end, Bhoyi's performance was a beautiful thing to see, full of nobility and humor and fierceness, without a trace of sentimentality, even though the events at the end of the play were dangerously melodramatic. Leleti and Seipati, in their roles of the poor twins Sweetie and Sweetheart, took the biggest risk of appearing precious or sentimental, but they avoided this. As Peter Brook had remarked about *Asinamali!:* "this horrifying situation was being presented, pitilessly, through a *joie de vivre.* The events were not softened by it, but heightened to the last degree because they were presented, not through a sentimentality, but through a vitality." And the fierce vitality was evident in every singer and every dancer up there, simultaneously honoring the struggle to live naturally and win freedom in South Africa, feeding their living relatives, and winning Mbongeni's favor. Behind the scenes, where it was so difficult to achieve Ali-like equilibrium, they may have squabbled and brawled, but they never seemed to differ about the nature of the work.

▼

In closing, I should not leave the impression that Muhammad Ali came all the way to South Africa just to see *Magic at 4 A.M.* He'd been planning a trip since before we'd met him in New York, to help promote a training center for underprivileged boxers in Durban. His visit had been scheduled originally for an earlier date, however, and it seems that the later date of our opening may have been a contributing factor in his decision to postpone. We had been in regular communication with Ali through his lawyer and through his best friend, Howard Bingham, for months and had received word that he was truly looking forward to seeing the play.

Ali had already been in the country for ten days, having arrived, with the timing of a true champ, on April 10, the day of Chris Hani's murder. On the front page of the April 11 Sunday *Star,* beneath a full-color photo of Hani's body lying bloodied in his driveway and the headline HANI KILLING: "I SAW MY DADDY DIE," there is a little boxed caricature of Ali and the line, "Ali, the greatest, hits town."

In the following ten days, he comforted the Hani family, consulted with Oliver Tambo—who died two weeks later—visited Nelson Mandela's old prison cell on Robben Island, received numerous tributes, attended many banquets, and toured all the hot spots of protest that blazed across the country. Another newspaper reported that in KwaMashu, near Durban, "he caused a security scare when he had his car stopped and joined a crowd of youths on the road. He then toyi-toyied [a protest dance] with them for close on a kilometre before the security men got him back into the vehicle." In Cape Town, the police refused to escort him to City Hall, where, according to the Sunday *Times,* "smoke could be seen rising from torched and looted shops. But Ali was not to be discouraged. He told his entourage: 'Choose: you can come with me or go back to the hotel. I'm going on.'"

When the opening-night performance ended, Mbongeni escorted an exhausted-looking Ali to the stage to join the company's curtain call. He stood awkwardly at the end of the line and waved to the audience, by now on their feet. Then, with his hands outstretched, seemingly in congratulations, he crossed to center stage, where Bhoyi was standing. But instead of a hug, he threw a shadow punch and danced from foot to foot, inviting Bhoyi to spar with him.

Ngema Family Name Praises

▼

Nina basengweni, nina bakwamuji, nina bakwasithenjwa, nina basemhlahlaneni, abakwaPhindisa, abakwamashiya, nina bakwamgabadeli abagabadela inkundla yakwaBulawayo. Bathi Madlokovu awungakanani ngoba uhlala entendeni yomkhonto intindinisane uhlale wenele. Hawu'ubani ongangawe sithenjwa na? Ngoba bathi wabonakala uqhamuka kumenyezwa kuthiwa, "Madlokovu sabela uyabizwa eNkonjeni, bathi woza uzobatshela izindaba zakubo kwaMalandela kwaZulu." Ehe' kunjalo nina bakwaPhindisa nina bakwamuji, nina baseMangadini nina bakwaNgema bakwaNene. Ho' Madlokovu amahle sibiza wena esimagqabhagqabha izingazi zamadoda. Goqo kaluzwiwa ngamatshe kephaluzwiwa ngamakhanda amadoda. Wena mxhazilothi zindlebe zikhanya ilanga khavukhavu Bambada imelika, ukuphi uma ukhona na? Nina bakwaphini elakhothwa munye ngoba ababili liyabasakaza nina bakwangqutu abanqutu zabanye abafazi. Siphungela, Madlokovu, uwena omkhulu ngoba khona kwaZulu inkosi yakwaZulu yathi uwuNgema ngoba wawengema wathi uPhindisa ngoba wawuphindisa umuntu uma ekhuluma okubi kuwena. Mu . . . ji, wena wakwaSiphungela ntusi yenkomo mashiya. Madlokovu.

Notes

PREFACE

INTRODUCTION

1 *A Woman Alone* (London: Heinemann, 1990).
2 *I Write What I Like* (San Francisco: Harper & Row, 1986).

CHAPTER ONE

1 *The Famished Road* (New York: Nan A. Talese/Doubleday, 1992).
2 *New York Times,* January 7, 1992.
3 Joseph Lelyveld, *Move Your Shadow* (New York: Times Books, 1985).
4 *I Write What I Like.*
5 *New York Times*, January 12, 1992.

CHAPTER TWO

1 *Chocolates for My Wife* (London: Hodder & Stoughton, 1961).
2 *Blame Me on History* (New York: Simon & Schuster, 1990).
3 Adam Hochschild, *The Mirror at Midnight* (New York: Viking Penguin, 1990).
4 Leonard Thompson, *A History of South Africa* (New Haven: Yale University Press, 1990).
5 *I Write What I Like.*

CHAPTER THREE

1 "The Discovery of What It Means to Be an American," *Nobody Knows My Name* (New York: Dell, 1961).
2 *I Write What I Like.*

CHAPTER FOUR

1 "Search for a Hunger," *Encore* 8, no. 4 (1961).

CHAPTER FIVE

1 "Kwashiorkor," *The Will to Die* (London: Heinemann, 1972).
2 Ibid.
3 *Chocolates for My Wife.*
4 Ibid.
5 Angus Wilson, "South Africa—A Visit to My Mother's Land," *Reflections in a Writer's Eye* (New York: Viking Penguin, 1986).
6 *Towards a Poor Theater* (New York: Simon & Schuster, 1968).
7 *The Empty Space* (New York: Atheneum, 1968).

CHAPTER SIX

1 *Black Boy* (New York: Harper, 1937).
2 Roger Southall, *South Africa's Transkei* (New York: Monthly Review Press, 1983).

CHAPTER SEVEN

1 Anton Chekhov, *Five Major Plays* (London: Oxford University Press, 1977).
2 "The Portuguese Sea," *The Penguin Book of Southern African Verse* (London: Penguin Books, 1989).
3 *Familiarity Is the Kingdom of the Lost*, ed. Barney Simon (New York: Four Walls Eight Windows, 1989).
4 Quoted in Pat Schwartz, *The Best of Company* (Johannesburg: Ad. Donker, 1988).
5 "The Social Function of Poetry," *On Poetry and Poets* (London: Faber and Faber, 1986).
6 "Joan Littlewood," *Profiles* (New York: Harper Perennial, 1989).
7 Schwartz, *The Best of Company.*
8 Ibid.
9 "Living in the Interregnum," *The Essential Gesture: Writing, Politics and Places* (London: Penguin Books, 1989).
10 Schwartz, *The Best of Company.*
11 Ibid.
12 Ibid.

CHAPTER EIGHT

1 *Woza Afrika!,* ed. Duma Ndlovu (New York: George Braziller, 1986).

CHAPTER NINE

1 *The Dramatic Imagination* (New York: Theatre Arts Books, 1941).
2 The meeting in 1988 was arranged by John Guare and the author of this book, co-editors

of *The New Theater Review*, a Lincoln Center Theater publication. This and following Brook quotes are taken from the published transcript of the meeting, which appeared in the *Review*, no. 3.

3 *Woza Afrika!*, ed. Duma Ndlovu (New York: George Braziller, 1986).

CHAPTER TEN

1 "After the Death of Mdabuli, Son of Mhawu," *A Land Apart*, ed. André Brink and J. M. Coetzee (London: Viking Penguin, 1987).

2 "Living in the Interregnum," *The Essential Gesture: Writing, Politics, and Places* (London: Penguin Books, 1989).

CHAPTER ELEVEN

1 "Chirundu," in *Voices from Twentieth-Century Africa*, selected by Chinweizu (London: Faber and Faber, 1988).

2 *I Write What I Like.*

CHAPTER TWELVE

1 *A Woman Alone.*

2 "Everybody's Protest Novel," *Notes to a Native Son* (Boston: Beacon Press, 1955).

3 "The Essential Gesture," *The Essential Gesture: Writing, Politics, and Places* (London: Penguin Books, 1989).

CHAPTER THIRTEEN

1 "Three Days in the Land of a Dying Illusion," *Call Me Not a Man* (Johannesburg: Raven Press, 1979).

INDEX

▼

DATE DUE

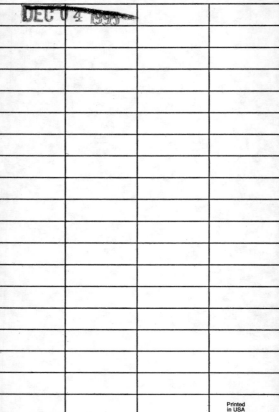

DEC 0 4 1995			
			Printed in USA